W9-DII-399

Twenty Years on Wheels

Twenty Years on Wheels

by

Andy Kirk

as told to Amy Lee

Discography compiled by Howard Rye

Ann Arbor
The University of Michigan Press

First published 1989 by The University of Michigan Press

1992   1991   1990   4   3   2

Library of Congress Cataloging-in-Publication Data

Kirk, Andy, 1898–
   Twenty years on wheels / by Andy Kirk as told to Amy Lee ;
discography compiled by Howard Rye.
      p.   cm. — (Michigan American music series)
   Bibliography: p.
   Discography: p.
   Includes index.
   ISBN 0-472-10134-X (University of Michigan Press : alk. paper)
   1. Kirk, Andy, 1898–   . 2. Jazz musicians—United States—
Biography.   I. Lee, Amy.   II. Rye, Howard.   III. Title.
IV. Title: 20 years on wheels.   V. Series.
ML419.K58A3   1989
784.4'165'092—dc20   89-33002
  [B]   CIP
                                                     MN
                                                      Rev

Typeset by Opus, Oxford
Printed in the United States of America

Publisher's note

The manuscript for *Twenty Years on Wheels* was produced by Amy Lee from transcripts of numerous interviews with Andy Kirk. To make clear the context of the story, the italicised sections for each chapter are Amy Lee's own words.

Inevitably, in a life story as long and varied as Kirk's, there will be incidents where his memories differ from other published accounts. The publishers are grateful to Howard Rye, whose work in preparing the discography has helped to establish the correct sequence of recording dates, and in editing the final text, this has clarified the order in which some of the events described occurred. In a few cases, Kirk's memories are at odds with this sequence, but these have been checked with him, and with other published sources. In particular, Frank Driggs's pioneering research has been helpful, notably "My Story by Andy Kirk as told to Frank Driggs", which appeared in *Jazz Review* Vol. 2, No. 2 (February 1959). In his separate introduction to the discography, Howard Rye draws attention to the use made of published interviews by other band members, and the publishers are doubly grateful to Mr Rye for having read and commented on the text of the book in the light of this information.

The plate sections consist of photographs drawn from Andy Kirk's collection, and are reproduced by permission. The author gratefully acknowledges prints made available by Vance Allen, Frank Driggs and Theo Zwicky.

The publishers are also grateful to Caroline Richmond for final editing work on the text and discography.

Contents

1   The first music I ever heard   1

2   I quit school in my sophomore year   17

3   "Ever think about playing an instrument?"   33

4   Twelve Clouds of Joy   50

5   The first big date in New York   68

6   Until the real thing comes along   81

7   Those wheels were still rolling   101

   Discography   120

   Index   144

1

The first music I ever heard

Say Kansas City.
And what's the next word?
Jazz.
And blues.

We were a Kansas City band known more for ballads than for blues. We came in from another place altogether. We brought in the Western and Texas influence. We played waltzes, too – Viennese as well as standard three-quarter-time pieces. Ben Thigpen never could get that Viennese beat – da-rrrmp, da, da – though he was a fine drummer, with me 17 years. His son, Ed, traveled with us before he was born.

Andy Kirk reached over and pulled out a clipping from one of the albums on the couch in the study of the Kirk apartment, 14-B 555 Edgecombe Avenue, New York City. Filled with band and family pictures, memorabilia, old itineraries, the albums were usually stacked neatly on shelves over the couch. But for our Sunday afternoon talk sessions, he had them where he could reach them easily.

Here's what the *Kansas City Call* wrote about Andy Kirk and his Twelve Clouds of Joy in 1933. "One of the best bands west of New York City, after receiving all honors at the Musicians' Ball at Roseland, at which time six nationally known bands were brought together." I had Pha Terrell then, singing ballads. Earlier we'd had Joe Williams, Count Basie's "Number One Son." He's closely identified with the blues, but I'd say Joe is primarily a ballad singer. You should have heard the way he sang *Lovely to look at* with us! Ballads were our big thing, but we played plenty of jazz, too. In our early Kansas City days Ben Webster was with us for a while, and later Lester Young. Lester had been with Fletcher Henderson, but his light sound didn't fit in with that band, especially after Coleman Hawkins and his big sound.

The Clouds had great feeling for one another. We went out socially together. We had a softball team. We enjoyed sports. Stumpy Brady, who had been an athlete – and still plays beautiful trombone, and without teeth – and Edgar Battle put on gloves one night, but I had a rule – no fighting on the bandstand – and Battle hasn't hit Stumpy yet. One thing Stumpy did tells you more about that feeling the Clouds had for each other. After he gave me notice to go with McKinney's Cotton Pickers he asked to stay on two weeks longer. He didn't feel he should go, with Mutton Leg – Ted Donnelly – not getting all the trombone notes quite right.

The study, third in a row of four rooms fronting on Edgecombe, seemed remote from the traffic moving noiselessly along the Harlem River Drive far below. It was September but still warm and the windows were open. The sounds of occasional buses stopping and starting again in front of the building drifted up faintly through the Sunday quiet.

Kansas City was often referred to as the "heart of America," because of being the city nearest to the geographical center of the United States. For us Kansas City was like the hub of a wheel with spokes that extended in all directions. From there we traveled the "spokes" on one-nighters to every state in the union except Vermont and crossed both borders into Canada and Mexico. I wrote a tune about those years, 1929 to 1949, and called it *Twenty Years on Wheels*.

His right foot tapping a gentle 4/4 beat, his right hand accenting the 2nd and 4th beats across his knee, Andy half-sang, half-talked the lyric:

> Twenty years on wheels,
> Just a-rollin' and a-rollin' and a-rollin',
> Twenty years on wheels,
> Moved with musical emotion and devotion
> From the heart of Kansas City to the north, east,
> south, and west,

We just kept rollin', hardly took any time to rest.
Twenty years on wheels,
Still believin' there'll be better times tomorrow.
Twenty years on wheels,
Sometimes running into trouble and sorrow.
But for the good times, the experience,
And the host of lovely folks we met,
I could never regret
That rollin' –
Twenty years on wheels.

Hold on, I'll give you a copy.

He eased his nearly six-foot frame from the chair, searched through a pile of music on a shelf behind it, finally pulled out a lead sheet and handed it to me. In the upper right-hand corner it read, "Lyrics and melody by Andy Kirk, ASCAP. Arr. by Ray Copeland." Andy sat down again, and, in a characteristic gesture, brushed his face with the palm of his hand, turned his hand over and ran it back under his chin.

The little jazz clubs on 12th and 18th streets in Kansas City stayed open all hours. People milled from one to another and sometimes went right on to a morning ball-game in their evening clothes. We often had early morning softball games in the park that ran from 15th to 18th street after the clubs closed around 5 a.m. – a good workout before going to bed.

But the first music I ever heard was a world away from Kansas City jazz clubs. It was in a Denver sanitorium, where Auntie was working as a cook. And it had the same effect on me then that Bennie Moten's swingin' blues had on me 20 years later. I'll show you Auntie's picture.

Andy drew the albums towards us and opened them. From their pages handsome Victorian faces of all shades, all ages – parents, grandparents, aunts, uncles, cousins – looked uncompromisingly out from their neatly assigned places under the clear plastic covers.
I leaned forward to get a better look and saw a face of determination and strong character.

I was born on 28 May 1898 in Newport, Kentucky, and named Andrew Dewey Kirk. My mother and father, Dellah and Charles Kirk, lived in Cincinnati, but mother was a Kentuckian and wanted her child born in her home state. Newport is just a mile across the river from Cincinnati, an easy walk – like walking across Manhattan island where it's a mile wide. More than one bridge connected the two cities. There was the L&N railroad bridge. There was another for horses and wagons, and trolley cars and pedestrians. Mother might even have walked across just before my birth. I was probably born in the home of one of her friends. My father contended that I was born in Cincinnati and many years later he pointed out the house where they were living at the time.

Our little family remained together just three and a half years, because my mother died at a young age – she was only 26 – from a sickness known in those days as quick consumption. Her half-sister, Mary Banion, adopted me because my father had left town and disappeared. I never saw him again until I was 32 years old. We were playing at Willow Beach, an amusement park by Maumee Bay on Lake Erie, on the outskirts of Toledo. I learned from his sisters, Virgie and Irene, that he was working at the Grosse Point Country Club. On our day off I drove to Detroit, and after I found the club I went in to enquire about him. I was directed to the men's locker room.

"I'm Charlie Kirk's son," I said to a man standing near the door.

"There he is, over there," he said, "talking to that man."

His back was to me. I went over, touched him on the shoulder, and said, "I know you're Charlie Kirk. I'm Andrew, your son."

He looked around, and dropped his head. When he got over the shock, he introduced me around: "This is my son. This is my son."

The three or four men in the room looked very surprised, then they shook hands with me and kept saying, "Well, Charlie, didn't know you had a son."

"Yeah," he said, "only one."

From then on we were very close. We had 30 years, from 1931 to 1961, the year he died, to get acquainted.

When Auntie took me in she was already a widow with three children of her own, all in their teens. Celeste was the oldest. Next was Rial Charles. She was a girl but had been named after her two uncles. She changed her name to Arcee. That was her way of spelling out her initials. The youngest was James Emmanuel – cousin Jimmy. I looked up to Jimmy. He was seven years older and always looking out for me, doing little things for me, like fixing my Christmas tricycle. I mention that because it's sort of a miracle how I got it.

I'd heard how Santa Claus came down the chimney and left presents by the fireplace. In our house there was no fireplace and no chimney. We did have a stovepipe in the kitchen, but I couldn't see how that big, fat, round man with his bag of toys could ever get down it. I told Auntie I didn't believe in Santa Claus. She didn't try to make me believe. She was a practical woman. She saw she could save a little money on me. "All right," she said, "you don't believe in Santa Claus. No toys."

Celeste was doing housework for the Mickey family – Mr Mickey was a jeweler in town – and sometimes she'd take me with her. The Mickeys had a son Billy, about my age, so we played together. That Christmas Mr Mickey gave Billy a tricycle. And he gave me one, too! We called them velocipedes in those days. Oh, how I loved that velocipede. I pedaled it for all I was worth around the neighborhood on the board sidewalks we had then – even over the rough, stony roads in Mays Lick, Kentucky, where my grandmother lived. That's where I broke it, the part that held the handlebars to the front wheel. Cousin Jimmy took it to a blacksmith and had him weld the two pieces on each side of the broken part. But it never worked successfully again. It hurt me to my heart when I broke it. That velocipede was the only toy I ever had, except a sled Jimmy made for me.

But I forgot my sorrow over that little three-wheel velocipede when the big iron wheels of the Missouri and Pacific rolled Auntie and me out of Cincinnati into Denver, Colorado. I was six. The year was 1904 and by then there was already a small colony of us colored folks in Denver. Mary

Banion had heard domestics were paid much higher wages in Denver than in Cincinnati. She got the news at church. That's where word of better jobs and pay was passed around as it filtered back from relatives and friends who'd gone west. Mary Banion knew what she was going to do. When Auntie made a decision, she'd go right at it – right now! She didn't fool around.

Auntie's and my first home in Denver was McKay's Tubercular Sanitorium at 425 Broadway, where she got a job as cook. It was moved later into what had once been a private mansion at East Colfax and Milwaukee. People had mansions at the turn of the century. In 1972 that mansion was still there, the only one left, standing among all the new businesses and steak houses. The McKays had moved to Denver from Mississippi because Dr McKay was a specialist in treating lung disease. People with that illness came to Denver sanitoriums from all over the country.

I "helped" Auntie with her work in the kitchen, stacking dishes and things like that, but most of the time I played out in the backyard and stayed close to the cook's quarters. The doctor didn't permit us to visit among the patients for fear of contagion. But sometimes I did go as far as the parlor door, where I could peek in and see Miss Janie, one of the patients, when she played the piano and sang the songs that were popular then and in the 1890s. I guess playing and singing were all she thought she had to look forward to. I didn't know it then, but Miss Janie got me hooked on music.

During the time I lived at McKay's with Auntie I went back to Cincinnati with a relative or someone, and came out next with cousin Jimmy. We couldn't all come out at once, it was too expensive, though of course I rode free. Jimmy was carrying a big picture frame. We'd always come out with things we didn't need. I was to be Jimmy's guide. I knew how to get around Denver on foot from walking with Mammy Hughes, my Uncle Jim Kirk's mother-in-law. Uncle Jim had lung trouble and had gone to Denver in the early 1900s with his wife and Mammy. Mammy was part Indian, and she walked a while!

Mammy had taken a sleep-in job with the Bromfield family on Emerson Street, so after we got off the train at Union Station we started for the Bromfield home about 20 blocks away. Mammy could tell us how to find Auntie. She and Celeste and Arcee were living near there, on Colfax. We struck out southeast from the station on 17th Street. Streets in the downtown section were laid out paralleling the South Platte River. I can name the streets we crossed as if I'd just walked that route: Wynkoop, Wazee, Blake, Walnut, Larimer, Lawrence, Arapaho, Court Place, Cleveland Place. Then we came to Broadway, which runs north and south. After Broadway we crossed Lincoln, Sherman, Grant, Logan, Pennsylvania, Pearl, Washington, Clarkson, and finally came to the Bromfield home.

Andy reveled in saying those street names. They evoked for him a happy childhood time, and for me a time edging the frontier, bringing an earlier America and the Indian presence suddenly close.

"Colfax and Auntie's house is not too much farther," I told Jimmy. Mammy put me straight. "No, Andrew," she said, "the Colfax you know is East Colfax, a block from here. But your Auntie's house is in the opposite direction, on West Colfax, west of Broadway."

I hadn't known anything about East and West Colfax, just Colfax. We walked back to Broadway and continued west across Acoma, Bannock, Cherokee, Delaware, Elati, Fox, and Galapago. There, near where Walton ended, was 727 West Colfax – Auntie's! She had rented the upstairs of a two-family house. Celeste and Arcee were both working as maids, so they could help with the rent. Many people had maids in those days. They paid them by the month and kept them on their payrolls, just the way offices keep typists and secretaries on their payrolls today. Auntie was taking in washing.

I couldn't hear Miss Janie sing anymore, but I had someone else to listen to: Arcee. She was an alto and could harmonize. I liked to hear her sing. She had been very close to my mother, and told me that one of my mother's favourite little sad songs of the 1890s was *She was only a bird in a gilded cage*. Arcee sang that to me more than any other song so I could know what kind of a person my mother was. They all did what they could to keep the image of my mother alive for me, because I hadn't known her. Arcee especially tried to plant the image of my mother in my mind.

The general sentiment of the times was with her. It was a period of mother worship. There was always a lot of talk about "mother." And all those songs – *Mother Machree, Mother's your best friend, after all, There's no one like mother to me,* and *A boy's best friend is his mother.* The more I heard all this mother talk, the more I began to feel sorry for myself. I could make myself cry. "Everybody's got mothers," I'd whimper, "except me." I used it as an excuse to get out of work. We were all given certain duties, the two girls, Jimmy and I. But sometimes when it was my turn to dry the dishes, I would conveniently go to sleep, and my aunt wouldn't wake me. My mother was her favorite sister, so she was especially nice to me. Jimmy was nice to me, too, even though he sometimes had to do my chores as well as his own. Everybody was nice to me. After a while I began to feel ashamed of myself for my schemes. I knew I was wrong. So I made the correction myself. Nobody else had to correct me. My own conscience whipped me.

We stayed only a short time in that house. The Fords, friends from Cincinnati, lived downstairs, but they must have thought I made too much noise upstairs. One day Mrs Ford started up the stairs after me to spank me. Auntie intervened just in time. She stopped her ironing, held up the iron like a fist, and said, "Don't you touch that boy. Any time he needs a whipping, I'll do it. Don't come upstairs. Just stay down there." Auntie was feisty.

We moved into a little one-family house at 630 West 14th Avenue, next door to an Irish family. They had two boys, so I had new playmates. Their father was a conductor on the tramway. Conductors, I found out, were very important people. They had charge of the tram cars. They walked up and down the aisles to collect fares and made change from the little metal coin holders attached to their belts. As soon as they got the right amount for the fare, they pulled a cord overhead to ring it up on the register at the front of the car where everybody could see it. Fare was five cents and you could transfer free.

In September 1905 I was enrolled in first grade at Longfellow School. I didn't have to go to kindergarten, because I'd had a lot of help at home learning words and counting. Arcee and Jimmy used to spell out syllables of words and pronounce them, like "p-r-e – pre, v-i-e-w, view – preview," and have me repeat them the same way. I was seven and ready for real school.

I got my first job when I was eight, selling "extras." The *Denver Post*, the *Rocky Mountain News*, and the *Denver Times* were always putting out extras – baseball extras, fight extras, extras for any big event – like the murder of the famous architect Stanford White, by Harry K. Thaw over Evelyn Nesbitt. That's how people got the news in the days before radio and TV. Any kid who didn't have a regular paper route could stand on a corner and sell. First one there would announce, "This is my corner," but there was always a lot of yelling and scrapping and even fist fights to establish territory. We all wore something like a dashiki made of unbleached canvas, with a pouch in front and one in back to hold the papers. When the front pouch was empty, we just turned the thing around so the full back pouch was in front and kept selling.

All the kids got in on selling the New Year's edition. That was the biggest extra of all. While the other kids were shouting, "Get your New Year's edition," I was shouting, "Get your New Year's position." I thought that's what they were saying. You developed your own sound. That was a selling point. People recognized it and they'd look for you. As soon as I went into my chant, "Read all about it. Get your New Year's position!," heads began popping out of front doors. "Oh, that's my regular boy. Hey, over here." I'd run up one front walk, deliver an extra and pocket the money, then run to the next house for another sale, and keep on like that up and down a whole block. Extras were five cents. We made two or three cents on every paper we sold. A dime bought a lot then. And it was "six picks for a nickel" at the candy store.

One news event I'll never forget – the Jack Johnson–Jim Jeffries fight on 4 July 1910. Jeffries had been heavyweight champion of the world and they brought him out of retirement to fight Johnson, but by then he was no match for Johnson. In those days news of all the big sports events came over the telegraph wire into the newspaper offices. That day, as news of the fight came into the *Rocky Mountain News*, they put up bulletins of each round in the big front window of the news building. Also a young lady took it down in shorthand, then three copies were made in longhand and passed on to me and two other kids waiting on our bikes for it. We'd ride with it in relays, pedaling as fast as we could down the eight blocks to Eureka Hall, where a matinee dance was going on. This way the crowd at the hall got round-by-round news of the fight – "hot off the wire" – even before the extras were on the street. Once the extras were out, I was selling them: "Get your prize-fight extra here. Johnson beats Jeffries. Read all about it."

One sports reporter on the *Denver Post* called Johnson "the big cinder" and always referred to his "inky hands." Johnson had been convicted originally for violating the Mann Act. And people didn't like it because he was married to a white woman. In those days that wasn't generally accepted. He got out of the country before sentencing. In 1915 he fought a match in Havana, Cuba, with Jess Willard. It was generally thought that he threw the fight to avoid prosecution in the US. Whether he did or not, he returned anyway and had to serve time. He was my one big hero. Years later, after we came to New York to live, we'd see him driving up Seventh Avenue in his Duesenberg, or notice it parked somewhere on a crosstown street.

Well, we moved again. Way over east to 3739 Williams Street, not too far from the Union Pacific yards. It took Auntie a long way from church. She had joined Zion Baptist, which was downtown at 20th and Arapaho. All the colored churches were in East Denver, but 3739 Williams Street was so far out east that we were 20 blocks from the action. It was a long walk every Sunday and Wednesday for prayer meeting. Sunday was a full church day. We had to be there at 9:30 in the morning for Sunday School. Church service was at 11. Then back at night for Baptist Young People's Union at 6:30 and another church service at 7:30.

I began hearing a lot more music, and learning hymns. One of my favorites was one we sang in Sunday School, *Let the blessed sunshine in.* Another I liked was *Abide with me.* We sang that in the church services. I liked singing with the congregation and listening to the choirs, especially the bass singers in the senior choir. One was our family doctor, Dr Anthony Wade Jones. The other was Mr Alex Waller, a real-estate man. I couldn't get enough of that bass sound. It was so rich and full and carried a lot of authority.

Our move to Williams Street brought me into a new school district, Hyde Park, where I was enrolled in third grade. Even in third grade I was already hard-headed about some things – like a silly game our teacher, Miss Leslie, liked to play. She would sit in a chair at the head of an aisle, and if you were chosen to be "guesser" you were supposed to kneel down, put your head in her lap, shut your eyes, and then guess how many fingers she would hold up. One day I was chosen to be "guesser" and to put my head in her lap. I rebelled. "I won't," I said.

"You will."

"I won't."

"Come up here," she commanded. "You're going to play this game like the rest of the children."

I went up, but I shook my head. "No, I'm not."

She was so angry she half pushed me out into the hall, closed the door behind us, and there she tried to trip me. But she stopped, almost too furious to know what to do with me. So she said, "You march right up to Mr Hatch's office!" Which I was happy to do. Mr Hatch was the principal. When I got there all he said was, "Sit down. Over there." He picked up some gloves that a delivery man had brought in and tried on a pair. He smoothed down the glove on his right hand, then held it up for me to see. "Doesn't this look like a good spanking glove?" he asked.

"Yes," I gulped, "I guess it does."

But instead of coming at me, he just looked at it some more, then began taking it off. He had me sit there in his office for ten minutes while he looked over the rest of the gloves. Finally he said, "All right, you can go back to your room now." He never asked me, "What are you here for?" or anything else. He must have known – and was probably on my side.

There was another incident, this time outside school, that made me realize you couldn't jump to conclusions about who your friends might, or might not, be. Late one afternoon Auntie asked me to go to the grocery at the corner and get a couple of things she needed for supper. On the way I met up with the Seastone brothers, white kids a little older than I was. Their father was umpire for the Sunday afternoon ball-games on the lot at 39th and Race, not far from our house and right on the outskirts of Denver.

But there was no umpire around to referee the Seastones versus Andrew Kirk. They grabbed me and began pulling my hair. It was kind of long and thick and woolly. And they knew how to pull it. While they were scuffling me around, all at once another boy appeared out of nowhere and pulled them off. He was an older white boy named Ben Davis. Like Mr Hatch, Davis didn't stop to figure my skin was brown and theirs was white.

Our family and the Garrisons were the two colored families in that neighborhood. Since Russell Booth Garrison and I were the only colored kids, we naturally got acquainted with the white boys, and the ball-lot was where kids usually got acquainted. Every new kid had to be tested, of course. When the testers found out I could throw a curve ball, I was in the big league. I was crazy about baseball. To choose sides it was hands up on the bat. The one with the last hand up – and how you'd squeeze to get your hand between the top of the bat and the closest hand – was winner and could choose sides.

Best of all, I had wheels again – a bike! Jimmy helped me get it. He had a Pierce, made by the Pierce Arrow car people. Mine was an Iver-Johnson. I was still riding it at age 22. You might wonder how a nine or ten-year-old could manage a bike big enough for a 22-year-old. For one thing, the seat was adjustable; it could be raised or lowered. Then I was tall for my age, and skinny, and I had long legs. My nickname – everybody had a nickname – was Slim. Bikes were made of heavy metal then, made to last, and I took care of mine.

Lots of times we went down by the tracks and jumped on the freight cars being shuttled around in the Union Pacific yards. We'd jump on one car, ride two or three blocks, then switch to another. That's where I acquired my first respect for wheels. I hopped a freight one day, but my foot missed the first rung of the metal ladder at the end of the car; it went between the rungs and hit the flange of the wheel. I hung onto that ladder for dear life, straining to keep my foot away from the wheel. At last the car stopped. I got off as fast as I could – and I haven't hopped another freight car since. I didn't tell anybody, either. This is the first time I've ever mentioned it. I'd have gotten plenty more than a lecture from Auntie, but I figured I didn't need a whipping. That close call was enough!

But not enough to stop me from riding on the steps of trolley cars. Trolleys had stationary steps before the kind that folded up when the doors closed. Sometimes I ran alongside a moving trolley and hopped on the steps. It didn't seem dangerous. And I was glad I knew how the day I got in a fight with a kid on a street corner. He was coming at me pretty hard, but I finally knocked him down – or he slipped. I was so glad to see him on the ground, I started to run. I saw a trolley coming, and before he could get up and chase me I hopped on the steps and rode away. "He who fights and runs away, lives to fight another day."

I could move fast when I had to, but Jimmy nicknamed me Grandpaw because I was usually slow and deliberate. Instead of jumping up from a chair, I'd just stand up.

Everybody respected Jimmy. He carried himself in a way that said, "If you want to speak, OK. If you don't, OK." By then he was 16 or 17, working age if you didn't go to school, and even though he was only 5'9", he never looked – or was – scared.

There were gangs on different streets and one day the gang that hung out on 30th and Franklin, a couple of blocks from us, came looking for Midge, a white boy in the neighborhood. The leader was Buzz Murphy. He later became a ball player with the Philadelphia Phillies. Shorty Dennison was his "lieutenant." "We're after Midge," they said. Gangs always said they were "after" somebody when they didn't like something about him. Midge must have been hiding nearby, because suddenly he ran into our house. Jimmy and I were the only ones home. "Get him out of there," Dennison yelled, and he and the gang started up the front steps. Jimmy moved to stall them off.

"You can't come in my home like that," he said, walking right into the middle of that gang. They backed down a step or two onto the walk. He moved towards them. Dennison said, "Well, can Buzz come in?"

Jimmy looked at Buzz and said, "OK, if you think you can find him."

Meantime Midge had slipped out a window into the backyard, jumped over the fence and disappeared up the alley.

It was that way Jimmy had. He and Russell Booth Garrison and I used to ride our bikes all the way up Williams Street till we ran into Grasshopper Hill, then up the hill to get alfalfa for the chickens to scratch in. It grew wild there. Wherever we lived we always kept chickens. That way we had plenty of eggs. It helped a lot. My aunt was born in the farmlands of Kentucky and would have been lost without her layers and fryers.

One time on our way to Grasshopper Hill we passed some white kids standing on a corner. One of them made a remark. Jimmy calmly stopped, rested the pedal of his bike on the curb, and walked right up to them. Russell and I stopped, not sure what was happening. "Which one of you said that?" Jimmy asked them.

There wasn't a sound. Not a sound till today. They chickened out. Jimmy was a game little fellow. He wasn't afraid of anything in the world.

We were occasionally called "nigger" by white kids. They'd yell at us,

> Niggy, niggy, never die,
> Black face and shiny eye,
> Crooked nose and crooked toes,
> That's the way niggy goes.

Those were fighting words. We'd settle it in the alley and be back friends again. The guy you were fighting might even be your best friend. There wasn't much prejudice in Denver, though it might come from somebody who moved up from Texas.

By the time I finished fourth grade – I skipped half of the third – Auntie had heard of a house to rent at 2435 Arapaho Street, closer to town and closer to church. We moved again. For me it meant a new school, Gilpin, and a new interest, boxing. Boxing was thought of then as the manly art of self-defense. After all, we settled arguments with our fists. We never thought of knives, or clubs, or stones. Or guns.

Jimmy was my boxing teacher. He taught me how to block and jab and punch, and how to feint. We had lots of challenges. One guy would put a chip of wood on his shoulder. We talk about people going around with a chip on their shoulder – well, this was a real one, a chip of wood, and he'd dare you to knock it off. You had to be ready to do it. We always fought a fair fight – the cheers and boos of the partisans gathered around to root for their champ.

Boxing was really an art, and good protection. I even made money at it now and then. There were two rival social clubs in our community. The one I belonged to was called the Eros Social Club. For recreation, among other things, we had boxing. The clubs held their tournaments in a big room at the back of Bill Lewis's grocery store on Welton Street. Bill was the first colored man in our neighborhood to own a motorcycle. We called him Motorcycle Mike after a comic strip character by that name. A friend of mine, Burkie Harvey, and I sometimes signed up to put on an exhibition boxing match at the club smokers. We learned how to pull our punches so as not to hurt one another. But sometimes we got excited and really mixed it up.

Besides professional boxers we knew about from newspaper stories, we had some local heroes. The main one was Jimmy Colston, my wife Mary's brother. We looked up to him because he was good with his dukes and was referred to around town as Young Gans. Joe Gans of Baltimore was about the first black lightweight champion of the world. I really admired Jimmy Colston. He was in the upper grades at Longfellow School when I was in first grade. I knew who his sister Mary was, too. She and her little friends used to ride by the ball-lot on their bikes when we were out playing.

2

I quit school in my sophomore year

It seemed odd there were no Andy Kirk recordings on the shelves or stacked by the record-player under the front windows in the study. "They're all stored out in New Rochelle," Andy explained, "in the attic of Fritz Pollard's house. I sold him that house when I was in real-estate here in New York." It was typical of Andy not to have his records at the ready. He never seemed overly impressed with his own success or with what others considered milestones on the way to it. Music, once he found it as his way of life, transcended all the career embellishments it generated. And it was time again to pick up on the Denver days.

In another year or so we began packing again. The expressman came, loaded our stuff on his flat wagon with the tailgate, started up the horse with a clap of the reins, and in no time drew up at our new address, 2516 Curtis Street, just a block and a half away. I could still go to Gilpin School. Gilpin seemed to be full of nice teachers. And music.

Mr Wilberforce J. Whiteman was supervisor of music for the Denver public schools. He had a son, Paul, but we didn't know him. He was several years older and by then had left Denver. No one that I know of had any idea that he would someday be THE Paul Whiteman.

Our Mr Whiteman was a small, slender man and wore a wax mustache. He always came to the class with his pitchpipe. He'd blow an A on it, and as soon as we had the right pitch we'd go into songs like *Santa Lucia* and *My country, 'tis of thee.* We learned to sing by ear. To learn the syllables of the scale – do, re, mi, and so forth – we watched Mr Whiteman's fingers shape the sounds and tried to work our mouths into the same shapes.

We sang Italian songs in English. We sang German songs in German because we were studying that language in school. German was a very popular language before World War I, and the German influence was strong. One went like this: "Der Christbaum ist der schönste Baum, den wir auf Erden kennen." Another we sang was "Hi li, hi lo, Ich bin ein Jägermann." We had a wonderful German teacher. She always greeted us, "Guten Morgen, Kinder."

"Guten Morgen, Fraulein Meschaus," we chorused.

I was also getting into performing. I sang with a Gilpin quintet that took part in Friday assembly and holiday programs. We were a mixed group: three girls (two colored and one white) and two boys (one white and me). For one program we were given a song to sing that I thought was derogatory. It was *Sleep, Kentucky babe*. I may have been a Kentucky babe myself, but I didn't want to sing about this one. I bucked it. We had to sing it anyway. When we got to the line after that humming phrase, "Lay your kinky, woolly head on your Mammy's breast," I rebelled and sang, "Uh-h-h-UHHHH!"

Miss Boyer, the eighth-grade teacher and assistant principal, called me aside. She reasoned with me, trying to make me see that this song was no reflection on me or the others of the quintet majority. "It's just a song," she said. "That's the way it was written, and you're not up there to be laughed at."

"OK," I said, but I really didn't like it. I liked her, though. She was always helpful and encouraging to me, but I knew she didn't really know how the kids with "kinky, woolly hair" felt about that song. We were sensitive about these things. Of course, it's not that way now. But most of the songs in school were fine. One I never forgot was a carol a white kid named Roland sang for a Christmas program. It was the prettiest Christmas song I'd ever heard, and that boy could sing:

> Praise the Lord in one accord,
> Him joyful homage pay,
> Age and youth proclaim the truth
> That Christ was born today.

I learned it after hearing him sing it.

For my Christmas piece that year I recited a little comedy thing in farmers' lingo. It was so different from the usual angels' wings flapping, that the kids broke up. It went

> Since Christmas Day has come and went
> Said Uncle Herman Gray,
> There's just a bit about it, folks,
> That I'm a-gonna say.
> Maw's long list of pretty things
> Cost me quite a bit of cash.
> Louise hit me for bric-a-brac,
> Besides perfume and such trash.
> Sue Anne cost me a signet ring.
> Now I ain't a man that knocks,
> But all that the gals and Maw gave me
> Was one cheap pair of socks.

School wasn't the only place for music. Denver itself was full of music. There were free concerts at City Auditorium. All the girls studying piano went to them. In summer there were band concerts in City Park. It was the time of brass bands. We went to all the parades to hear the bands. The *Denver Post* sponsored a boys' band, but it was just for white boys. There were minstrel shows at the Empress Theater, but some of us looked down on them. We felt they weren't up-building.

One time I had a chance to sing in a 40-voice children's choir Mr Whiteman organized for a concert in the new pavilion at the Civic Center. The center was a majestic place. At the eastern end the State Capitol stood atop Capitol Hill. At the western end was the United States Mint, and near that the main branch of the Denver Public Library. I felt good singing there.

Noticing my interest in music, Auntie decided I should have piano lessons. A piano was part of the furniture in those days. We had a Hamlin upright which Arcee used to play a little. I didn't want to take lessons. As far as I could see most piano students were girls. But to please my aunt – she thought she was doing me a favor – I started taking lessons from Miss Beatrice Thrashley. She came to the house once a week. Lessons lasted an hour and cost 50 cents. I even remember one little exercise. But while I was thumping around on the exercises and pieces, I could hear the kids yelling out on the ball-lot and the crack of the bat on a pitcher's fast ball. I had a hard time keeping my mind on *The Happy Farmer*.

Finally Auntie saw what was happening. "I'm not going to waste another cent on you for music lessons," she said, "since you aren't going to practise. And that's final." I didn't argue with her. I had a couple of other pressing engagements – playing second base for our Sunday School team and riding tailgates all over town with Herb Walker.

Herb was quick, kind of Irish, puggy, and always getting me into things. Once he even made me fight a kid in our class from England to settle *his* quarrel with him. I thought of him as a daring character. I also thought he was a white kid, but some people said he was a mulatto. He was brought up by a light-skinned black couple, officially his parents. His "aunt," a white woman, came to see him every once in a while and brought him money. She paid the black "parents" to bring him up. There was talk, but no proof, that she was really his mother. I was big enough by then to see there was something going on, but, whatever it was, it didn't affect us kids.

Herb left Denver when we were in high school. But he came back once after a stretch in the navy. He came to see me and stayed overnight at our house. He had some cock-and-bull story, said he was on his way to California and needed a little cash. I knew him by then, but I was working, so I gave it to him. Several years later, when I was playing the Paramount Theater on Pershing Square in Los Angeles, who should come backstage one night but Walker. We shook hands and he said, "You're a fine one. I wrote you a letter, and you didn't even let me know you'd gotten the money." I said to myself, "The nerve of this guy." I knew he never sent me any money or any letter.

We moved again, to 2420 Emerson Street, right around the corner from Zion Baptist. Auntie could get there in a minute and a half. I didn't do too much contributing to the spiritual welfare of the church. I got baptized when I was ten or eleven because the other kids did. I'm pretty sure I didn't know exactly what I was doing. But we had a wonderful Sunday School teacher, Luther Walton. All the kids loved him. He even bought uniforms for the Sunday School baseball team. He arranged a program of picnics one summer and had something going for us all year round. He was like a scoutmaster. I looked on him as a father. Incidentally, in those days there were only two main sports, baseball and football. Girls played a little basketball.

But life for me wasn't all riding tailgates and playing ball. It was school every day and working. Ever since I was eight and started selling extras I'd had lots of little part-time jobs, so I always had something in my pockets to jingle. In the winter I stoked furnaces. Summers I cut lawns for 25 cents a lawn, and picked dandelions out of the golf course at Denver Country Club for maybe 50 cents. Weekends I had a special kind of job for the Jewish families who lived around the corner from us on East 24th and on Ogden. They owned most of the little neighborhood shops and grocery stores where we traded. We were steady customers at Rifkin's grocery. You could pay your bill at the end of the month. Even after we moved to 2410 Marion Street we still traded with Mr Rifkin, and eventually he built a new store on the corner lot right next door to us.

The Rifkins and the other families were orthodox Jews and observed the sabbath very strictly. They could not do any work on the sabbath, which was Saturday, so my job was to make fires for them every weekend. Friday nights I gathered up newspapers and kindling and laid the fires in their kitchen coal ranges. Saturdays, just before sundown, I would get the fires started for them. Once the sun had set their sabbath had ended, and they were free to cook and carry on their work as usual. The Bible says neither you nor your manservant nor your maidservant shall do any labor on the sabbath, so they put the sin on me. I bore it for them. For 15 cents a fire I didn't mind.

Years later I ran into the son of one of those families at Crawford Music in Chicago. I'd known him as Izzie, but he had Americanized his name for business reasons.

For a while I had a part-time job after school in the office at Morris Coal and Feed in the neighborhood. As I was getting still taller and stronger, Mr Morris soon put me on the wagon delivering coal in small gunny sacks, the size I could carry. Coal was 25 cents a gunny sack, $4 to $5 a ton, lignite and bituminous. At home we'd get a ton of bituminous and a half ton of lignite. I liked the bituminous. There was so much heat in it and not so much ash. When it broke you could still see the shape of it. It didn't break into fragments. There were a lot of mines up in the mountains outside of Denver – silver, gold, and bituminous coal.

One of the biggest scares came the day I had Celeste's three-year-old son, Orville, with me on the wagon. Celeste had married a man named Scott Slaughter and was very proud of her little son, but it was Auntie who really raised him. Orville and I were sitting up on the high seat, the kind with those elongated springs underneath. We'd been out quite a while and I knew the horse would be thirsty. I pulled over to a watering trough. Just then he shied at something and stopped suddenly. Orville pitched forward and fell right under his hind legs. "No!" I yelled, and that was one time I moved fast. I jumped down and pulled him out before the horse could step back. It was a close one, but he wasn't hurt, thank goodness! I didn't tell anyone, especially Auntie. I was too big to whip, but she would have had a good tongue-lashing for me. But she never knew it.

The move to 2420 Emerson put me in the Whittier school district. With only half a year to go before graduating I wanted to stay at Gilpin. The law was, though, that when you moved into a different school district you had to get special permission from the superintendent's office to stay in your former school, and you had to have a reason that made sense. I thought I had one. I was getting ready to go to high school. Miss Boyer and two other teachers had offered to help me make up the work I needed to get out in half a year.

Because I had skipped half of the third grade I had to make up a half of eighth grade to graduate in June instead of the next February.

The superintendent of schools gave me a permit to stay at Gilpin. I went to see Mrs Houghan, the principal. She didn't waste time or words. "You're going to school where you belong," she said, meaning Whittier. I was only 13, but I had my thoughts about that. I left her office and went to see the principal at Whittier. And who should it be but Mr Hatch, the former principal of Hyde Park School who had spared the "spanking glove" and taken my side in that silly game episode.

I explained my situation and showed him the permit. He didn't waste time, either. He reached for his pen and wrote a very short note. As I was standing right in front of his desk I could see what he wrote. "Mrs Houghan, please obey the superintendent's orders." Period. In 20 minutes I was back in her office with the note. She read it. "Oh, yes," she said. "Go to your room."

I had to do a lot of cramming to get through the regular and make-up work. But with those wonderful teachers helping me, I had to make it.

One morning, several weeks after I'd been doing all that extra studying, I overslept and came in late for school. The teacher said, "Andrew Kirk, get your things and go. . ." She paused. I was scared. I thought she was going to say, "to Mrs Houghan's office." Then I heard the rest of the sentence. ". . . and go to room 20." That was Miss Boyer's room. Eighth grade. It was my special promotion. All the kids clapped. I graduated with the class in June 1912.

Talk at dinner drifted to improvisation. Andy mentioned emceeing a program at Charlie Colin's 1975 Brass Conference for Scholarships at New York's Hotel Roosevelt.

It featured members of Westbury, Long Island, High School Stage Band. And what were those kids playing? *AK Blues*. That was a head thing our band put together years ago. Those kids were demonstrating how well they could improvise after a crash course in Ray Copeland's *The Creative*

Art of Jazz Improvisation. I told Mary afterwards how strange it seemed that kids today "take" jazz improvising in school.

Mary said, "I thought jazz improvising was something you felt, not something you could learn." She knew plenty about it from her own piano-playing days in Denver, including stints with George Morrison's top band, and later with her own little groups in Kansas City.

And that's true. But even when you feel it, you have to have models to imitate at first, to get ideas from. At least those kids had the help and inspiration of a great black jazz trumpet man and arranger like Ray.

I had to get my first jazz "instruction" from white musicians, and certainly not in school. I don't recall we'd even heard the word jazz then. We had heard of ragtime, and various ragtime artists came through Denver from time to time. I remember one number called *The Dance of the Grizzly Bear,* because we made up parodies to it the way we did to all the popular songs. Our favorite on *Grizzly Bear* was the one we made up for Jack Johnson, the great black heavyweight champion of the world. It went like this:

> Get up close to him, Johnson,
> Knock his head against the ceilin',
> Make him have a funny feelin'.
> Put that twist on him, Johnson,
> Close your eyes and start nappin',
> Something nice is going to happen.
> Put that shift on him, Johnson,
> Knock him ever-y-where.
> Show your darling girl
> That you're the champion of the world.
> Johnson's the grizzly,
> I say, the grizzly,
> Johnson's the grizzly bear.

The word jazz didn't become widely known, as I recall, until Paul Whiteman introduced Gershwin's *Rhapsody in Blue* at Aeolian Hall in New York in 1924. That made jazz "respectable." But *Rhapsody in Blue* and the Whiteman style of music were only what was generally thought to be jazz. The jazz I heard in the little Kansas City jazz clubs couldn't have gotten within miles of a concert hall – then. It was in those little clubs where musicians from bands like mine got "educated" in jazz and blues. They were our school. That's where we learned improvising and got ideas.

The summer after I graduated from Gilpin I got a job as a bellhop at the St James Hotel. I was only 14 but I could pass for older because I was tall and slender. I worked alternate shifts: one day, 12 noon to 6:00 p.m., the next day 6:00 a.m. to 12 noon, and back at 6:00 p.m. till midnight. My salary was $25 a month – you could get a room at the hotel for $6 a week – but I averaged $7 a day just in tips from miners and cattlemen who stayed there and didn't put any value on a dollar. They came in to Denver to spend their money at the theaters and restaurants and night spots. The three main hotels – the Albany, the Brown Palace, and the Oxford – had music for dancing.

Denver was the biggest city in the area. The others were Pueblo, about 120 miles away; Cheyenne, Wyoming, about 100 miles; and Salt Lake City, Utah, 500 miles away.

As I said, I always had something in my pockets to jingle, but I'd never seen this much money before. In fact, I was making so much I was late enrolling in high school. There were four high schools, all taking students from the various grade schools. I went to East Denver High. At the same time Willie Smith, who became the alto sax star of Jimmie Lunceford's band and later went with Harry James, was at South Denver High.

Right away I had trouble with algebra. My six-week mark was a D, so I had to take two algebra classes, the regular one and the make-up. Again I had help from the teachers. Denver schools did everything possible to help you. There was no prejudice among the teachers. I worked that D up to four A's, the only honor I ever got, and I never got an A after that. I wasn't interested. I was thinking more about working. I'd been working all my life and I had no parents with schooling to urge me to get an education. I could always get jobs, and I thought it would always be like that. And it was.

The first few weeks in high I took my lunch in a lunch box. I was a skinny kid and always ready to eat. One day I opened my lunch box as I was coming down the front steps of the school. All of a sudden I was accidentally struck from behind by two white kids. They picked me up and said, "Are you hurt?"

I said, "No." My lunch had gone flying. I couldn't even see where the box had landed. They asked me if I had any money with me. I shook my head. For some reason I had none with me that day. They took me across the street to a little cafeteria and bought my lunch. I never forgot that. I doubt if there was really much prejudice among most of the white students.

There was just one colored boy on the East Denver High football team. He played halfback. Everybody at school loved him, but when our team played other schools, then it was rough. He was the only colored high-school player in the city, as I recall, so opposing teams wanted to see him hurt and get him out of the game. He had to be outstanding, and he was. We called him Socks.

There were 50 of us colored folks in an enrollment of over 1700 at East Denver High. And we were seldom in class with one another. We segregated ourselves, always sitting in a row together in assembly.

We did have quite a jolt one Friday when the high-school glee club sang a number they called a folk song. These were the words:

> Went down to the river,
> And couldn't get across.
> Jumped on a nigger
> And thought it was a hoss.

Our jaws went out. The other kids giggled and looked to see how we were taking it. I was pretty angry and started to walk out. But Bryce Woodard, who was sitting next to me, caught me by the sleeve and said, "Wait. We'll go see the principal afterwards." I agreed, and when the program was over we caught up with Mr Barrett, the principal, in the hall and told him we had something to talk about to him. "Come on in the office," he said.

He listened to our complaint and said, "I wouldn't be upset. People sing songs about the Irish, the Jews, the Italians." He tried to smooth it over that way. "But if you object," he said, "I'll see that it doesn't happen again." And it didn't.

Things like that taught me not to hate all white people just because one called me a nigger.

And I got valentines from the white kids in class, some I didn't know even thought about me at all.

And a really big event happened for our household. Auntie bought a house at 2410 Marion Street, a two-storey, seven-room brick house, with a hot-air furnace. It was a larger house than we'd ever lived in. The front door opened onto a hallway, with stairs at the left leading to the second floor. The living room was at the right, and beyond it the dining room. The dining room windows were bordered with panes of colored glass. Beyond the dining room was the kitchen, and off that a small bedroom. At the head of the stairs a right angle turn led to my room. Across a little hall and farther down was another bedroom, and at the end of the hall the bathroom. Auntie had the large bedroom next to mine that faced Marion Street. The house had a small yard and a barn in back. I tore down the barn myself and built a chicken house.

The summer after my freshman year I answered an ad that said, "High-school help wanted for thinning sugar beets on homesteading property in Deerfield, Colorado, about 75 miles out of Denver." Sugar-beet farming was a growing industry in the state. There were sugar-beet factories in Brush and Fort Morgan and other little towns near Deerfield. What I didn't know was that the ad specified high-school help because it was cheap. I went up by train, wearing a good suit, but I had a pair of overalls with me. That's what we worked in. They were the dungarees of that day.

The land we were to work on had been granted by the

government to black homesteaders. They had to work it at least five years, as I recall, then it was theirs. It was baked-dry land, so there were big trenches that held water for irrigation, and a main trench with little gates that opened to let the water into the rows of sugar beets. We got up at 3:30 a.m. and worked all day, sunup to sundown, for $1.50.

There was a "boss" of each row – called himself a bell cow – who went ahead, singing and chopping, setting the pace. Those bell cows kept us in line as we worked our way down the rows. We had to go on our knees, working with a short hoe to thin out the beets the width of the hoe. We padded our knees, but I guess my pads weren't thick enough because my knees were skinned from dirt clods. The heat from the sun was fierce. There were very few trees. Maybe a few cottonwoods along a small brook or two.

We lived in a barracks-like building. For food we had old salt pork and potatoes fried in salt-pork grease. They did give us an egg occasionally. But the main food was salt pork and fried potatoes. I got sick of that job in a hurry and quit. I put on my suit again and walked to one of the small stations where they switched trains and asked a brakeman, "Going to Denver?" I explained the only money I had was a small check on a Fort Morgan bank and a couple of dollars change. "Come on," he said, "get on," and let me in a freight car. I hoboed into Denver dressed up.

That hard-baked soil has changed. It's all green now. I saw it from a Union Pacific train when Mary and I were traveling to the coast from Chicago in 1960. You know the Bible speaks of making the desert blossom like the rose. That is just what has happened there.

I went into my sophomore year still working part-time jobs. At the St James Hotel I cleaned the lobby every morning before school. One of my after-school jobs was at Regal Shoe as a porter and delivery boy. Shoe stores and millinery stores always hired boys with bikes to make deliveries. The department stores made their deliveries by horse and wagon, later by Ford trucks.

Ben Davis, the white boy who had rescued me from that scuffle with the Seastone brothers, was a hopper at Denver Dry Goods, one of the city's big department stores. Hoppers made the rounds on the delivery wagons. After dropping off a package, they would run back to the wagon, which was already moving, and hop on the polished brass hub of one of the wheels, then climb inside. I preferred my own wheels.

I was always singing around the house, or outside with my friends. Jeff Johnson, who lived two doors down from us, was my special singing partner. Every night we'd be down at the corner under the arc light harmonizing on *Sweet Adeline* and *By the light of the silvery moon*.

I was enjoying more and more music at church, too. Cantatas like *Samson et Delilah* – I wanted to know what "et" meant. I never heard a sweeter sound than the soprano singing, "Oh, so happy," and the chorus with its responses.

The Azalia Hackley Choral Club saw to it that we never lacked for good music. Miss Hackley taught voice and put on pupils' recitals at Zion Baptist and the other black churches. Every spring Shorter AME Church was packed for concerts by George Morrison, the very talented black violinist and orchestra leader. His programs included pretty semi-classics and some popular songs. He always played a violin solo. One of my favorites was Fritz Kreisler's *The Old Refrain*. Mr Morrison played it so beautifully you felt it way down to your toes. And the way he played those double stops amazed me.

And to top it all there was a pianist named Blind Boone, from Missouri, who made the circuit of the churches every year. Everybody was on hand for Blind Boone. Methodists would jam the Baptist church, and Baptists the Methodist, to hear him. He played classics and ragtime. And he had a very special talent he liked to show off for us. After his program he would invite someone from the audience, usually Helen Minnes or one of our other local pianists, to come up on stage and play. As soon as she finished her piece he'd sit down at the piano and play the same piece, note for note, just the way she did. It brought the house down every time.

And a group I never wanted to miss was the Rocky Mountain Athletic Club Quartet. Rocky Mountain was a social club that went in for both singing and athletics. Every time Tom Berry, the bass, sang, "When the bells in the lighthouse ring ding, dong," and he'd go wa-a-ay down low, the rest of the quartet leaned over to watch him and make sure he hit that bottom note. Some with *Asleep in the Deep*. I couldn't get enough of that bass sound. It carried authority.

But I fell out with the church because of the inconsistency I saw there. Zion Baptist at one point had an educated preacher, a Yale man. The kids thought he was great. He had Bible studies with us. He spoke our language. The older people didn't like him. They thought he was talking down to them. I remember in one church meeting he said something that ruffled a few feathers, and one of the bonnet-wearing stewardesses got up and shouted at him, "You're a black liar."

Incidentally, the word black then had a derogatory meaning. The word black as it's used now, of course, came into fashion with the militants – Black Power, Black is Beautiful – the African heritage. I don't like the word. There are so many different shades. I'm not black.

I didn't think the preacher had said anything wrong. That made me realize there was a lot of anger in that church. I said to myself, "If this is love, I don't want to see it."

When I got home, my aunt, who wasn't at the meeting, noticed my long face. "What's the matter?" she asked.

When I told her, she said, "That should have made you fight more for what you thought was right."

Instead, I left. I thought it was wrong for Christians to have that anger. They should be having love for each other, not hate and fighting. I didn't go in that church again until my aunt died in 1953. I was 55 years old.

I was always for unity. That's why I would not have any fighting in the band. Oh, arguments, yes, but not to get that hate going.

High school was making me ask myself some questions, too. I had been reading in an English publication Auntie brought home – she worked for a while for a lawyer and his family, and whenever Mr Irwin threw out any of his old books Auntie brought them home. Anyway, I was reading about how a butler should propose to the housekeeper. I thought that butler–housekeeper idea was stupid. But then I saw we had the same kind of set-up here.

People I looked up to for a while were chauffeurs for rich people or butlers for congressmen. Our US senator, Senator Phipps, who lived in Denver, always took some of his servants with him to Washington when the Senate was in session. I thought that was a big deal. Millionaires' servants in Denver were considered the elite of the colored community. They had a recognized social club called the Bon Vivants. All the men working for rich Whites as chauffeurs and butlers copied the aristocracy. I had a chance to observe them when Jimmy was in the Imperial Comus Club and I was checkroom boy and on the door.

Harry Greinitz, who used to study with me at my house when we were sophomores, later got a job in an insurance company I never could have gotten. Incidentally, he sold me my first insurance policy, a 20-year endowment. Even in my sophomore year I knew there were certain jobs for colored people, so what was the sense of going to college to shine shoes or run an elevator? Our thought was to get out of high school and find something to do. I didn't see any sense in over-educating myself to be a waiter on a dining car. I quit school in my sophomore year, and began working full-time for Regal Shoe. Later I got a job as hall boy at the West Court Hotel. I kept those halls shining! Uncle Ben, my mother's full brother, took care of the court and lobby.

I had been going with a girl who was a friend of Mary Colston's. We'd meet over at Mary's house. Mary lived at 2327 Downing Street in a nice area. I could stand on our porch and see part of her porch, and I could run over there in three minutes. Then I started turning my eyes on Mary. We began going in the same group to little house parties around the neighborhood. And it just sort of happened.

There was a piano in nearly every house and someone to

play it. Mary and Frank Barnes always played, but they weren't the only ones. There were so many we had continuous music. One pianist would carry on from another. The one going off would be playing with the right hand while the next one was coming on playing with the left.

Mary's house was the best one of all for parties. It was open to everybody and a home where everybody enjoyed himself. Mrs Colston said, "There's no fun you can have away from home that you can't have here." Christmas morning the kids always gathered at the Colston house. And Christmas was when I'd go with Mary to her church, the Methodist. It was a little more modern than the Baptist.

I was crazier than ever about baseball and in a game nearly every Sunday. In those days various cigar companies sponsored ball clubs. These clubs played on corner lots and passed the hat at games. Auntie, being a "hardshell Baptist," didn't approve of playing baseball on Sunday. That was wicked, very wicked. I had to keep my uniform at Bolder's Barbershop on 19th Street, between Champa and Curtis, where I'd pick it up and then go and join the team. Though I was no longer a churchgoer, I still had respect for Auntie's home and tried to govern myself accordingly.

Later I played with a semi-pro team, the Maple Leafs. We played other teams in the city league.

3

"Ever think about playing an instrument?"

The furnace at 555 Edgecombe, which had been out for several weeks, was finally working again. Outside the cold January wind whipped at the windows, but the study was warm. Andy was saying again what he said so often.

My greatest advantage was to have lived in Denver. We were not recognized as equals, but we did have equal opportunity for education. The schools were all open to us. There was no such thing as "you can't go to this school." Teachers in the Denver schools – even probably Miss Leslie in spite of her silly game – were outstanding. They were qualified. And they were *people*. They wanted to do a job and see results in the kids they were teaching. They saw to it that we learned. We had to go through all the exercises to learn how to speak the English language. German, too, as I mentioned earlier. As a result, we could speak it and we could read and write. And if you didn't show up at school, a truant officer was at your house to find out why.

The Denver teachers helped us from the heart. Their attitudes helped me to keep away from black and white entanglements all the rest of my life. Out there we had clear thinking. We had nothing to cause us to think any other way. I love Denver for that reason. I thank God for it.

Of course, when I was in school, from 1905 to 1914, there were no black teachers in the school system. But now George Morrison's kids, Marion and George Jr, are both teachers in the schools there. And in 1973 George Jr became principal of my old school, Hyde Park, which now has a new name as well as a new-style principal.

All this points to a change of times. We've had doors opened to us that were closed when I was growing up. But the thing I remember so strongly is not so much the prejudice – I had a taste of that – but of people extending themselves to help me. All of this stayed with me. And I realized that color has nothing to do with anyone's personality, either black or white. In my time of growing up and in my experience I found that to be true, so I can speak with authority about it.

But back to 1916 – and to a welcome change in my routine. In the 12 years we had lived in Denver, Arcee hadn't been back to Cincinnati for even one visit. She wanted to see her grandmother, Winnie Hathaway, and her great aunt Amanda, Winnie's sister. And Aunt Allie Bolden, my mother's full sister. Both Winnie and Amanda had been born slaves. Amanda was the sassy one. She lived out the last years of her life in Wheeling, West Virginia, and every time our band played in the area I'd go to see her. She must have appreciated those visits, because in her will she left what she had to two nieces and me.

For an anniversary present Arcee's husband, James Goff, gave her a six-week vacation in Cincinnati. One snag – he couldn't leave his work to go with her. Could Andrew? What a chance for me to get re-acquainted with both my grandmothers – my father's mother in Cincinnati, my mother's mother in Mays Lick, Kentucky, where long ago I broke my velocipede!

I'd been working steadily in the two years I'd been out of high school. I was 18 and wanted to feel those train wheels rolling under me again. I quit my job at the West Court and took off with Arcee. We had to change trains in St Louis, so we decided to stay a few days with a Mrs White. She'd been visiting Denver to get the mountain air and we'd all become friends.

One day we went to see a black ball-game at LaClede Park, the St Louis Giants versus some team in the National Negro League. Another day we took in a vaudeville show at one of the TOBA theaters. That was the negro equivalent of, say,

Keith for white theaters. I don't remember any of the actors except one comedian named Slim – my old nickname.

We had a wonderful time in Cincinnati and Mays Lick renewing family ties. Wherever we were invited, or we went calling on neighbors, Aunt Amanda went with us. She had no children of her own, so Arcee and I were her family while we were there. I also had one very important mission, to buy clay pipes for Mammy Hughes. She hadn't been able to find any in Denver.

Back home again, I got a job as an elevator operator at Denver Dry Goods on 16th Street. 16th was the main business street. All the department stores were there – Golden Eagle, Daniels and Fisher, A. T. Lewis and Son, Joslyn, the May Company, and a couple of ladies' wear stores. One was Neusteter. Across the street was Gano-Downs, a well-known men's store distinguished by a rather startling innovation in design, a concave window. I hear they still have it, and it's Joseph Magnin's now.

As soon as Mrs West of the West Court Hotel found out I was in town, she tried to get me to come back to work at the hotel. I gave her some excuse as to why I couldn't. The real reason was I was stepping up. The job at Denver Dry Goods was a dress-up job. I wore a sharp baby-blue uniform and the job demanded some skill. There were three elevators – two for passengers, one for employees. The employee and no.2 passenger elevators were electric. The no.1 passenger elevator was hydraulic, propelled up and down by water power. To run it you had to take hold of a big handle fastened to the floor just inside the door. And you had to work that handle from side to side, just so, to get the elevator cab even with the floor at every stop and keep it under control.

This is what took skill. You could learn little tricks to make it look even more skillful. Showmanship. For instance, if the elevator should creep a little at a stop, I would steady it by keeping the arch and heel of one foot inside the cab and placing my toes on the floor outside. Control with a subtle bit of showmanship. We liked to turn everything into show business.

I liked operating the hydraulic elevator, but I liked being on the employees' elevator even better because I could sing and whistle on it. There was a new piece I was crazy about called *Poor Butterfly*. The pianist at Knight-Campbell music store had played it for me one day during my lunch hour. Music stores and stores with music departments all had pianists to play the latest popular pieces for customers. No buying a pig in a poke. I sang and whistled *Poor Butterfly* on that elevator for days!

The war in Europe was heating up. We were in it now. Our first troops had landed in France on 26 June 1917. Manpower was getting short at home. The store began putting girls on the elevators and shifting the men operators to porter and window-washing jobs. I had to train a girl to operate the hydraulic elevator. She was doing all right as long as I was there showing her just what to do. But on the first trip by herself she threw the handle over too far and too suddenly. That started a momentum that took the cab up fast and brought it to a sudden jolting stop. In this kind of situation the cab would be still going up from the power, but the cable it ran on would be slack, so the cab would bounce up and down. That girl was so frightened she let go of the handle and grabbed her ears. I had to take the handle and get us back down again.

But once she got the hang of it I was switched to washing the store's big plate-glass windows on 16th Street. I didn't mind it but there was no show business in it. There was show business in shining shoes, though, as I soon found out.

Arcee's husband had been working out of town and wanted to come back to Denver to be with his wife. He recommended me for his porter and shoe-shining job at Jay's Barbershop in Sterling. Sterling was 139 miles northeast of Denver and, in old railroad terminology, the first division out of Denver going to Chicago. They changed engines there.

The barbershop, owned by Mr Jay, a cripple and a fine old man, was on the main square in the center of town. It was a nine-chair shop serving Whites. I had to go to Denver to get my hair cut. And get over my lonesomeness. I was paid $6 a week, but made much more, with tips. It was that showmanship in how you used the shining rag and brush. You'd draw the rag its whole length across the shoe, then pop the rag and draw it back the other way, all in rhythm. Every shoe shiner could think up his own patterns. You could even imitate the sound of train wheels rolling over the tracks. Then you'd brush off the customer's coat with a whisk broom, in rhythm, like a drummer swishing his wire brushes on the snare of cymbals.

The war was driving prices up. A five-cent shine had shot up to 15 cents, and on a Saturday did we turn 'em out. All told, I was averaging between $40 and $50 a week.

You could learn the truth about both Blacks and Whites working closely with them. I met some interesting people – my regular customers were businessmen in the neighborhood and we'd talk while I was shining their shoes. One customer baffled me. He always looked nice, dressed well, and was always smiling. But, oh, how his feet smelled! I couldn't see why so well-dressed a man should have such odorous feet. A barber told me, "He's coky. Sniffs cocaine." That was the first time I had ever seen anyone who used dope.

Some of the barbers had outside jobs. One worked for an undertaker. One played tuba in the Sterling Municipal Band. I soon joined the moonlighters. The manager of a hotel around the corner gave me a job meeting trains. There were two a day. Salesmen from Denver came up to get orders. The hotel manager furnished me with a two-wheel cart to haul baggage. With my pay, plus tips from the travelers, I was adding still more to my weekly take. Tips often came to $5, and $5 then bought a lot of food.

I ate in the restaurant a couple of doors up the street from the barbershop. I would go out the back door of the barbershop and into the back door of the restaurant to eat in the kitchen. It was the only place I could be served because of the restaurant's rules. It was their way of life.

Most people then thought Blacks were afraid of their shadow. The barber moonlighting for the undertaker asked me to come over to his boss's funeral parlor one night. He wanted to show me around. I suppose he thought he was going to see my hair shoot up like he'd seen in too many movie comedies. He *knew* Negroes were scared of the dead and of ghosts, so he suddenly drew the sheet off one corpse and looked at me, as if he expected to see what he'd seen in the funny papers. I gazed calmly at the corpse and said, "Who is he? Poor fellow."

One rainy day business was slow at the shop. There were no shoes to shine, so I began browsing through a music catalogue that belonged to the tuba-playing barber on the ninth chair. When he finished with his customer, he looked over at me and asked, "Are you interested in music?"

"Yeah," I said. "I like music."

"Ever think about playing an instrument?"

"No, I hadn't thought much about that."

He talked a while about the various instruments and said, "Well, if you ever decide to play one. I suggest you buy a saxophone. It's new and getting very popular." He showed me a picture of one in the catalogue. I had seen George Morrison's trombone player doubling on C-melody sax, but it hadn't moved me. "It's easier to learn than most instruments," he said. "You don't have to develop a lip like for the trumpet or trombone. It's a reed instrument, and it's really a novel instrument in America. It was invented in Europe by a German named Adolphe Sax."

The more I listened to him, the more I wanted to try one. It would be something to do evenings. There were only seven colored folks in town. I didn't know them and they didn't know me. They were working. I was working.

I discovered that Seymour's Drugstore, just a few doors from the barbershop, sold instruments. It was the local agency for Lyon and Healy, the harp-maker and musical-instrument firm in Chicago. Seymour's happened to have a B-flat tenor saxophone in stock. It was made of brass and I bought it for $75. Paid cash.

I lived upstairs over the barbershop in a kind of loft, furnished with just a bed. People could take a bath at the barbershop for 25 cents. I took mine free. Now that I had my new saxophone the barbershop took on a whole new dimension. As soon as the shop closed at the end of the day, I would pull down the shades and practise before going up to bed. Mainly I just wanted to blow away some of the loneliness. I knew how to read music so I concentrated on learning fingering from the instruction book. On Sundays when I didn't go to Denver I practised some more.

The tuba-playing barber on the ninth chair kept encouraging me. He talked to me a lot, told me about embouchure and reeds. "Try out reed number so-and-so till you work up an embouchure," he'd say. He had explained that embouchure meant the way of using lips and muscles to play the instrument. "Then try another number reed. It'll come to you which one you feel most comfortable with." The music department in the drugstore helped me, too.

Finally I became so involved with the sax that I decided to give up the job in the barbershop, move back to Denver, and go into music.

I came back to Denver with my horn in the spring of 1918. On 28 May I turned 20. Too young for the first draft, which took men 21 to 31. I needed a job. On my way downtown one day I ran into James Russell, an old friend from Luther Walton's Sunday School class at Zion Baptist Church. He was wearing a sharp uniform, a letter carrier's.

"How'd you get that job?" I asked him.

"Took the exam. A lot of colored boys took it and got appointed. They're drafting so many men the post office has lost a lot of employees. They've got this special exam for replacements. "Go down to the post office," he urged me. "C'mon, I'll go with you and get an application."

A month after taking the exam I was notified I'd passed and was given a special classification – 3G. I was appointed a letter carrier and called to work in August. I was subbing on Joe Montier's route. One of the stops was the Whiteman home. I never saw Mr Whiteman and his pitchpipe, but I did see Mrs Whiteman once in a while and their daughter, Fern. Mrs Whiteman was a big woman, Fern of medium build. Incidentally, prevailing Denver opinion considered Mr Whiteman and Fern the best musicians in the family. Besides being superintendent of music for the schools, Mr Whiteman was choir director at one of the churches and Fern sang in the choir.

As if all the walking I did as a letter carrier wasn't enough, I added more mileage playing tennis in City Park, a beautiful oasis 26 blocks long. It had manicured lawns and sand roadways, a museum of natural history, a zoo, and six tennis courts. We'd get up about 4:00 a.m., ride our bikes to the courts and play as many sets as we could get in before work. We had to be at the post office by 6:55. After 6:57, a demerit.

Subbing as a letter carrier also meant doing Sunday collections. Late Sunday mornings I went around to the livery stable to pick up a US Postal Service wagon and horse and made collections from noon till four o'clock. There were two special horses everybody wanted. One, a sorrel, was fast. I called him Blitz. The other was slower but he was sensible. He knew every mailbox in town, and would stop at each one without a "whoa" or a tug on the reins. And instead of wearing himself out walking straight up Capitol Hill, he zig-zagged back and forth across it, making the top with ease. Sensible.

I liked horses. But we didn't have them too long. Ford trucks came in and mail collections had a new dash about them. But I missed the horses.

I had found an excellent saxophone teacher, Franz Rath, a former clarinetist with the Boston Symphony. He was in Denver because a member of his family who was in ill-health had been advised to move there. His son Walter later played the organ at the Isis Theater in town. Mr Rath encouraged me to use what I was learning. "The thing you should do, Andrew," he'd say, "is to get with an orchestra. Practical experience is the best thing you can have."

But I was kind of shy. When people asked me to play I'd make excuses and say, "Oh, I'm just learning."

One night after supper the front doorbell rang and I went to answer it. A man I didn't know stood there. "Are you Andrew Kirk?" he asked.

"Yes."

"I hear you have a saxophone."

"Yes."

"How'd you like to play at my hall?"

I was stunned. "Well, but – I just bought the sax a little while ago. I'm just learning it."

He was persistent. "But you *own* it?"

"Yes," I said, "I own it."

"Well, I'll pay you $4 a night if you'll just come and let the people see it. Weir Hall, on the north side. Can you come tomorrow night?"

I took a deep breath. "Well, OK, if you're sure that's all you want me to do. I can't play yet. I've just started studying."

"That's all I want. See you tomorrow night. Around nine."

The four-piece band at Weir Hall was just finishing the first set when I walked in, sax case in hand, feeling like anything but a lucky musician who'd been handed a job without even looking for it – and a job that didn't require him to play! I walked slowly along the wall towards the bandstand. I recognized Frank Junior Jr, the leader. He played banjo. (The other instruments were piano, drums, and trombone.) He spotted me and motioned for me to come up. I looked around. There were already quite a few people in the hall. Drawing back my shoulders, I went up on the stand and began unpacking my horn.

All I did that first night was just sit with the band and hold the sax, so people could come up and look at it. They looked *plenty*. Every time they danced by, they'd stare. If they asked questions about it, I'd say, "I just bought it." The B-flat tenor sax was something very new and different indeed, and mine was the first to appear in Weir Hall. The two or three other saxes around town were C-melody horns.

I was hired for two nights a week. That meant $8 pay. Riches. Bread was five cents a loaf, milk with thick cream sitting on top of it, eight cents. Just holding the sax for all that money bothered my conscience. I started playing whole notes and half notes, following the chord progressions, so I could feel I was playing with the group, doing something to earn that eight bucks.

My study with Rath was going pretty well, too. I soon graduated to "real" playing in different little spots around town, usually with four- or five-piece bands. I did gigs regularly with R. S. Williams, a banjo player, who played for lots of little private club affairs.

Meanwhile the draft had been extended to include men 18 to 45. I was reclassified 1A. But before they got to me the war ended. The Armistice was signed on 11 November 1918. When the whistles started blowing I was on the 3700 block on Gilpin Street, delivering mail. I threw all the letters in my hand back in my bag and started for the post office. When I got to 16th Street I saw a line forming behind a band in front of the *Denver Post* building. I joined it. I never saw so many happy people in my life. The war was over, the war that was to end war – to make the world safe for democracy.

I continued to carry mail. It was considered high class to work for the US Government. People were very patriotic then, and they thought any government job was the ultimate.

I was always taught that because of Abraham Lincoln I should vote the Republican ticket. That's all I heard from my relatives. But we were then under the Wilson administration. The Democrats were in power. A Mr Kelly was superintendent of mails and Ben Stapleton postmaster. You could go to Mr Stapleton any time with a problem. His door was always open. I found that out when I had occasion to seek his help during the tramway strike. I then had a fine three-tripper – three deliveries a day – in a semi-business section. Normally we rode the tramway on special post-office checks. When the strike was over we were supposed to return the unused checks to the post office. I had to go see Mr Stapleton and tell him I didn't have mine. "What did you do with them?" he asked.

"I don't know," I said, and that was the truth.

He gave me a little lecture on responsibility, then took time to ask about my personal life. "Are you married?"

"Not yet. I hope to be soon." He wished me well and let me know he wanted to meet his employees on a personal basis, that it was not just a cold business relationship.

In the Harding administration the postmaster and top men were changed. And, to me, the Republican postmaster was not nearly the man that Stapleton was. I learned that a man's character should not be judged by his politics. Later Ben Stapleton was elected mayor of Denver two different times.

Besides carrying mail I was still pursuing music. When I went into this music business I went in for the whole thing. I was studying arranging with Walter Light. I even took voice lessons. I learned how to breathe from the diaphragm. I knew my range: I could go from G to Z-flat. I joined Local 753, the black local, of the American Federation of Musicians.

I saw, too, that the more instruments you had, the more jobs you could get. Need a saxophone player? I'm available. Need a bass player? I'm available. I had also joined the Elks Lodge. The Elks had a marching band but no sousaphone player, so I bought a sousaphone for $250, studied with Alex Horts, and marched with the Elks. Next I got a string bass. I had to have a truck to carry around all my instruments.

Then the gates of Paradise opened: George Morrison hired me – on bass. He was playing at the Albany Hotel, one of the best in Denver. Morrison had a sweetish style but also a beat. His orchestra was versatile. It could move easily from one-steps and two-steps into the schottisches and waltzes and light classics his society clientele demanded. His ideal was Art Hickman, then a big name in dance bands, because his society followers liked Hickman. He had only one real competitor in Denver, a white bandleader by the name of Lohman who was also a violinist. Morrison knew all the big people, he was friendly with the owners of the *Denver Post*, and he played innumerable dances and parties in the homes of wealthy society people. Many were in city or state politics.

My greatest experiences as a sideman were with George

Morrison's band. When I joined Morrison in 1919 he had a woman, Jessie Andrews (later Jessie Zackarey), on piano. He ran to women pianists, perhaps because Denver had so many good ones. In time, one of his busiest and best was my girl, Mary Colston. Another was Desdemona West, who married Morrison's alto sax man, Leo Davis, of Kansas City.

Davis also played a Buffet tenor, a French make he had picked up while he was with the army in France. He could make it sound like a cello. When we played country-club banquets that cello sound was just right for the trio and quartet performances of *A Bowl of Pansies* and other light classics Morrison featured. Davis played soprano sax, too. I had acquired a bass sax, along with my tenor and the other instruments, so he and I used to do a very life-like imitation of Gallagher and Sheen with our soprano and bass saxes.

In 1920 the band made a trip to New York, mainly to augment an orchestra going to Europe. But when Morrison discovered his name was not to be up in lights, so to speak, he reneged on the Europe part, but we stayed in Manhattan to make records for Columbia. Through Tim Brymn, who had had a band in France during the war, we were also booked into the Carleton Terrace at Broadway and 100th Street for six weeks.

At this point I was getting less enthusiastic about string bass. While we were in New York – though I was playing tenor in the band – I noticed that string bass didn't record too well. The recording horns of those times couldn't pick up the sound. I had been studying the Hause–Franke System of Bass Instruction. With that you had to finger the bass as you would a violin. Other bass players I'd seen were going up and down the strings in their own way. I used a German bow – the hand is under the bow instead of over it as with the French bow. I didn't like that too well, though it was probably OK for symphony work.

Tubas were all around. I became more tuba-minded. But I had the string bass along with my saxes and tuba on jobs for display, if nothing else, until a fellow borrowed it one night. I never saw it again, and I gave up string bass for good.

All through 1921 and 1922 I was carrying mail. You couldn't moonlight on a post office job. But I did, playing my horns. Even if it had been permitted, carrying around those heavy mail bags every day discouraged it. But I was young, I could do both. We got off at 4:30 in the afternoon. I'd rush home, eat, and get to the job. Usually, about halfway through the evening, I'd nod and catch myself, and come in a beat behind.

I remember one job we were playing at Lakeside Amusement Park. Mary Colston was the pianist that night. I was sitting near the piano. One of the postal inspectors was there and he made a point of Peabody-ing elaborately around the bandstand and grinning at me, as much as to say, "See, I'm looking at you. I'm seeing you." I kept my eyes on the music as though I didn't see him.

I was also fighting to keep awake. Pretty soon I began to nod. Mary had a pitcher of water with a chunk of ice in it beside her on the stand. No ice cubes then and no electric fans, just the breeze from the mountains or the lake. Whenever she'd see me nodding she'd dip her handkerchief in the pitcher of water and hand it to me, to wake me up. She was always a helpmeet. When I was learning the tenor sax, I used to take it over to her house and she'd play the piano along with me, give me little pointers, encourage me.

George Morrison, too, encouraged everybody he thought had any talent. He made an arrangement of a waltz I'd written and played it, and he taught me things about arranging. He was patient with us. He never said anything about mistakes at the time you made them, but afterwards he'd say, "I knew what you were doing." He wanted to help you develop your talent, give you a chance.

I was also hearing things in bands that came to the Orpheum Theater that influenced my playing – bands like Isham Jones, Ted Lewis, Waring's Pennsylvanians, Ben Bernie. There was a tenor man with Bernie who was my first big jazz influence. His name was Jack Pettis. I even copied some of his solos.

After Paul Whiteman became famous as a bandleader he

and the band came to Lakeside Amusement Park in Denver for one night as a special attraction. It was George Morrison's regular job but his night off. Mary and I were both playing with Morrison then, so we all went to hear the Whiteman orchestra. Chet Hazlitt was on first alto sax, and a tremendous attraction for me was Ross Gorman, who played all the saxes.

I don't remember hearing or seeing any colored bands, except once when Happy Gene Coy and his Black Aces came up from Texas to play at the colored amusment park. They sounded very different to our ears. A lot of their tunes were original. Some were built on the structure of the blues. They had a good beat, and most of their tempos were slower than ours. We played schottisches and waltzes, one-steps and two-steps. And read music. There were three clefs – bass, tenor, and treble. I learned to transpose right away. We got the stock arrangements of every new tune that came out. In fact, we were playing stocks before they had sax parts written in them. When I was playing tenor with Mr Morrison he would have to give me the cello parts. Sometimes I played the second trumpet parts. I was so happy when Leo Feist came out with stocks that had sax parts. I think he was the first publisher to do so.

There was one other black music influence in my life at that time: Jelly Roll Morton from New Orleans. Like other traveling piano players, Jelly worked his way around the country playing the joints or wherever he could pick up a job for a night. On trips through Denver he often played with a George Morrison unit. Morrison had so much work he might have two or three bands going the same night.

One night I was playing tenor in a small Morrison combo at a little place up in the mountains outside of Denver that was used for an ice house. Jelly was our piano player. Just before intermission I called a number, a one-step named *June*. It had a Peabody tempo, sort of fast, and had the dancers almost running around the hall. During intermission Jelly said, "That's a good piece, but you ain't sayin' nothin'. Man, you gotta stomp it!"

After intermission we stomped it. But we couldn't keep it up. It wasn't our style. Jelly and his stompin' influenced me, though, and showed up in patterns I used later in arrangements for my band.

Between mail and music and seeing Mary there wasn't time for much else, but I did belong to a social club called the Thirteen Club (for 13 members). We wore garb like the Klu Klux Klan, except our robes were black and had a white 13 sewed on the back. The club's main purpose was gambling. During one session I was on a winning streak, but I had a date with Mary and was anxious to leave. The others were mad because I was winning and wouldn't stay longer. They thought my luck would change. I said to myself, "If I can lose friends like this, I'm going to quit gambling." I never gambled again. But I stayed in the club and my Model-T truck became the commissary truck, transporting food and supplies for club picnics.

In 1922 the Morrison band hit the road again, this time heading west. We were hired as part of a package, including trapeze artists and clowns, to play a string of Shrine and Elks indoor circus dates in Salt Lake City, Omaha, Phoenix, San Francisco, Los Angeles, San Diego, and El Paso. The circus was held in city auditoriums and arenas, or Shrine temples and Elks Lodge buildings. After playing for the circus acts we always moved to a cabaret setting in another part of the building and entertained and played for dancing.

At one of the circus performances we came close to seeing a tragedy as a couple of the trapeze artists were concluding their act. Leo Davis had already started for the cabaret, and instead of walking around their net he thought he'd save time, and walked under it. The girl, who was just about to throw the swing to her partner, saw Leo, and grabbed her throat. Her partner lost his timing and fell into the net just in time to graze Leo. It stunned him, but he recovered faster than his saxophone, which was bent and knocked up considerably.

We got that tour because of our showmanship talents. Hattie McDaniel was on it with us. She sang and recited poems by the great black poet Paul Laurence Dunbar. She stopped the show in every city we played. Her brother Sam was in movies, playing Pullman porter roles. Many times later, in the late 1930s and early 1940s, we stayed at Hattie's home in Los Angeles. She had bought a house with five bedrooms and five baths for $10,000 – equivalent to $85,000 or more now. It had a special heating set-up that permitted heat to be turned on in any one room according to the occupant's preference.

On this tour, while we were in Los Angeles, some of us went to a little after-hours club to hear the Quality Four. Henry "Tin Can" Allen played a kazoo in a tin can, Harvey Brooks was on piano, Leon Hereford on alto, and Paul Howard on tenor. Howard later became an officer of Local 47 in Los Angeles.

We ended the tour in El Paso, Texas, then stepped across the border into Mexico and took a job at a nightclub called Latino Americana in Ciudad Juárez. We played opposite a girls' band. Kids were always hanging around, their hands out, begging, "Uno centavo, uno centavo." I learned to count in Spanish because we were paid in Mexican gold coins and we wanted to be sure of what we were getting in the American equivalent. In 1922 a peso was worth 50 cents in American money.

One night a customer sent his card up requesting me to come to his table. On meeting him I was a little shaken to find out that he was a postal inspector. Before the start of the band tour I had asked for leave of absence from the Denver post office to go to California to be with my aunt. After all those years as a widow, Auntie had finally married again and moved with her new husband to the coast. He had gone out there to get work. But not long afterwards he was killed in a freak accident. A car had gone out of control and come up on the sidewalk where he'd been waiting for a bus, and struck him.

My leave hadn't specified circus dates or nightclub gigs in Mexico. After the postal inspector invited me to sit down and have a drink, he asked me, "Don't you intend to go back to your job in Denver?"

"Oh, yes," I said enthusiastically. "I'm going back tomorrow!" It was true. We were heading out of Juárez for Denver.

When I got home and reported to the post office I found they had a welcome-home present for me: 500 demerits. I had to show them that I really wanted to work. They gave me a little extra territory to be sure I'd have enough to do – 540 stops.

But I kept on moonlighting with George Morrison just the same. Mary and I also played one job at Rock Rest, I remember, with Jimmie Lunceford. Even then he was showing signs of the professor and strict bandleader he was to become.

4

Twelve Clouds of Joy

As I came down the hall towards the Kirk apartment, I heard piano music. It stopped when Mary let me in. She was practising the music for a forthcoming dance recital. The piano was in the foyer of the apartment, to the right of the door as you came in. Soon the music began again. The sounds drifted into the study, pleasant accompaniment to Andy's words.

In the summer of 1924 a 16-year-old kid named Alvin "Fats" Wall came to Denver from Little Rock, Arkansas, to spend his vacation. He had brought his saxophone with him. I soon met him. We always knew who was coming and going. We were a pretty close-knit community, what with only 6000 or so of us in Denver's population of about 300,000, and we segregated ourselves to be together. As soon as I heard this kid play I recommended him to Mr Morrison. He hired him for our fall tour of the Pantages vaudeville circuit.

We were heading west again. The tour kicked off in Minneapolis. From there we traveled through California to Vancouver, then south through Washington, Oregon, and California, then headed back east. We wound up at the Pantages Theater on 12th Street in Kansas City in May 1925. I don't remember much about the weather, but I'll never forget the heat from Bennie Moten's five-piece band at a little after-hours club on 18th Street. It was the first time I'd ever heard a band like that. It was *swinging* – playing the blues, all kinds of blues. Naturally, my ears were on Moten's tenorman, Woodie Walder. Tenors have always been important in jazz. The voice of the instrument has always had so much to say. If you notice, more tenors are talked about in jazz than altos. Incidentally, *A Mellow Bit of Rhythm*, which my band recorded, was written by Woodie Walder's younger brother Herman and Mary Lou Williams.

The summer of 1925 meant wedding bells for me. Mary Colston and I were married on 22 July in a ceremony at Mary's house, the house that had always been the best for parties in our high-school days. It still was. During the reception I got word that members of the Thirteen Club were going to kidnap me and keep me away from my bride that night. I disappeared into the kitchen, put on my own 13 hooded robe, which I'd left there after a picnic the week before, and got out through the basement and over to the Douglases' house two doors away. The Douglases were old friends. They had been our neighbors when we lived on Emerson, and they had arranged for us to spend the first night of our honeymoon at their house.

Once inside, I stood behind the glass panes in the front door and thumbed my nose at the frustrated "kidnappers" gathered outside. I wasn't much of an actor, but I played this scene to the hilt.

The bride and bridegroom left the next morning to spend their honeymoon in Colorado Springs, 65 miles from Denver. Big deal. In no time we were back at work.

I took a job at Estes Park with Frank Junior Jr. Leo Davis had married Desdemona West a couple of years before, and they were both in the band. Gene Montgomery was on drums. Estes Park was 8000 feet above sea level, 85 miles from Denver. We had then what were called shelf roads that wound around the mountainsides. There were no guard rails. Driving had to be in low gear all the way down. But I went home every chance I got to be with my new bride. We worked every night till 4:00 a.m. Clouds at that hour hung so low they often blotted out the road altogether. Sometimes we went through them. Sometimes they were below us.

Going home one early morning after work, Frank Junior and I met a car from Iowa coming up. It ran us off the road. Our car was caught in a tree jutting out on the mountainside, its rear wheels hanging out in space. We were shook up but unhurt, so we got out and dropped down on the slope where we could get a foothold. The Iowa car and another car we flagged down when we got up to the road pulled our car back on the road and we drove on into Denver.

In all my years on the road, criss-crossing the US in cars, buses, and trains, I was in only 14 or 15 accidents, none serious.

That fall Mary went to work with a small band at The Boulevard, a quiet kind of club on Colorado Boulevard in Denver. Frank Junior's group, with a slight change in personnel – Lester Grant on piano and Stewart Hall on C-melody sax – went into the Moonlight Ranch, a roadhouse owned by Mike Rossi out on Morrison Road, towards the mountains. The Moonlight Ranch was pretty high class for a roadhouse. Roadhouses were the thing then, a part of the scene. They were low and spread out, like dance pavilions, not like the architecture of clubs in town. There'd be booths along the sides, tables near the dance floor, the band set up at one end. Dim lights. Romantic, but also kind of dangerous. They were not for kids. Kids then were disciplined. Even school teachers could discipline them. Roadhouses were for adults because there was drinking in spite of prohibition. It was up to a grownup whether he wanted to risk jail or not. The marshalls usually had tips on who was making liquor. I'm pretty sure none was sold on the premises of Moonlight Ranch. While we were working there, at least, the place was never raided. Those who did the drinking had to bring their own flasks.

Roadhouses all had bouncers. Rossi had been in the Italian army and had developed his own brand of discipline. He acted as his own bouncer and let everyone know that he and his place were to be respected.

One night a man came in looking for his wife. He got into an argument with her and became a nuisance. Rossi warned him to quiet down, but the man paid no attention. Rossi then began beating him up: he had shown no respect for the club. The wife cried, "Stop it. That's my husband."

Rossi said, "Sorry, lady. I see no blood. Yet."

We saw plenty of action most nights, even blood sometimes. Mostly jealous husbands tracking down their wives' lovers. But the band stayed clear of these contests. We had our music to tend to. Our repertoire was made up mainly of pop tunes of the day, Berlin things, and we still played some World War I songs like *My Buddy* and *Over There* – tunes the people knew and liked.

The place was always jumping when Jack Altieri came in. He had been lieutenant in the Dean O'Banion gang. After it was broken up by rivals, Altieri retired to the mountains near Denver. He was still a hero in that club. Word always got around when he was expected. The place would be packed. Money flowed.

Rossi may have been tough with disrespectful customers, but he was always marvelous to the musicians, always had a little smile for us. Some nights he would ask the band to stay another hour or so after closing and play for a private party. The main idea seemed to be to give the girls a chance to show off their dancing. One man in the party would say to a girl near him, "That girl across the table from you said she could dance better than you. But I'm puttin' my money on you." Then the one with the money on her feet would get up and strut her stuff. They were all high on alcohol and would just twist around and do some nothing kind of dancing.

Usually we played till four in the morning, then went into the kitchen for breakfast – spaghetti and hot peppers!

We made it unscathed through the winter of 1926 and the next summer at Moonlight Ranch. In September Fats Wall came back to Denver from Canada, where he'd gone with another Frank Junior group. We saw an ad in *Billboard* for an alto man and a tuba player wanted by an orchestra leader in Chicago, and decided to answer it.

We rolled out of Denver on the Union Pacific in the late afternoon and got to Chicago early the next morning. I'd been through Chicago on that trip to New York with Morrison, but this was my first stay there. The guy putting the band together suggested places for us to live. I found a room at 3608 South Parkway with a lawyer and his wife, Mr and Mrs Hinton from Louisville, Kentucky. They were fine people and made me feel right at home.

Fats and I rehearsed with his ten-piece band for a couple of months, but nothing happened with it. I picked up gigs at Warwick Hall, a ballroom on East 47th Street, with a group called the Society Syncopators. Fats got a job with Charlie Cooke's Ginger Snaps. Cooke was a black bandleader well known in the Chicago area. About that time he got his doctorate in music and changed Ginger Snaps to Doctors of Rhythm. Years later he became one of the staff arrangers at Radio City Music Hall in New York.

Mary's sister Bernice was living in Chicago then, so I got in touch with her as soon as I could. She introduced me to several musicians she knew. We spent as much time as possible at the Vendome Theater. Erskine Tate was playing in the pit. Besides being a fine jazz group – Louis Armstrong had just joined, and Earl Hines was on piano – Tate's band had violins and flutes and played all types of music. They opened every show with an overture. The high point came, though, when they switched from the pit to the stage and showered down with some jazz. Bernice knew many of Tate's men well, particularly Norwell "Flutes" Morton who, obviously, played flute, as well as sax, and Charlie Harris who played oboe and sax. They were key men in performances of *Poet and Peasant* and *William Tell* and works of that type.

Fats left Chicago before I did. He'd gotten a wire from T. Holder – the T. was for Terrence – a trumpet player who had left the Alphonso Trent orchestra in Dallas to form his own band. Trent was playing at the Adolphus, a major Dallas hotel, at a time when there were to my knowledge no black bands in similar hotels in the North. George Morrison's long engagement at the Albany Hotel in Denver was the only comparable engagement I'd known of for a black band.

I soon got a wire from Holder, too. Fats had recommended me. When I arrived, Holder already had his first job lined up at the Ozarks Club just outside Dallas. What impressed me even more than the fights that went on nightly at the Ozarks, another down-to-earth roadhouse, was the expert marksmanship of the Texans in a little contest called Feedin' the

Kitty. All of us were familiar with kitties. They'd been on various bandstands in Denver. But I saw that feedin' the kitty in Dallas was very different from feedin' it in Denver. The feeders in Texas seemed to be richer and they were full of self-assurance.

We always put the kitty near the band's front line. It was a metal horn shaped like those old Victor talking machine horns, and set up on a box. Shoot a silver dollar into that horn and would it rattle and clank! One of the musicians would throw a silver dollar in to get things going. People in the audience would follow suit. Texans liked competition. When one threw in a dollar, another would toss one in with a look that said, "You're not gonna make a piker outta me!"

At the end of the evening Holder would say, "C'mon, mens" – he thought that was the plural of man – "let's count up the kitty," and the band would split the profits. Might come to a couple of dollars apiece extra. Good pocket change.

Those Texans were also intrigued with my accent. I was the only Northerner in Holder's band and did the Texans ever make fun of the way I talked! "He has to have a drink of wat-tah," they'd mimic. The way they said it in their Texas drawl was "drink of wah-h-hr." My northern accent broke them up it was so different.

I was absorbing new musical influences with Holder. And for the first time I heard Southwest-style jazz. Sunday afternoons we went to a dance hall called the North Dallas Club, where a bunch of very talented kids played Sunday matinees. One was Budd Johnson, who later took his tenor sax and Southwest jazz far beyond the boundaries of Texas. Another kid sax player in that group was Booker Pittman, grandson of Booker T. Washington. There were two fine trombone players, Keg Johnson, Budd's older brother, and Dan Minor.

Holder's band was a ten-piece outfit – three brass, three saxes, four rhythm – with a swinging beat and a good sound. I was growing more and more interested in the band as a whole, and was willing to give any help I could to make it better. Our trombone player, for instance, had a beautiful tone and could memorize easily, but he was a little slow on reading – he could spell. When something came along that he had trouble with, I'd pick up my bass sax and play the trombone part so he could hear it and that way get it in his mind.

I also did whatever writing was done. Holder didn't have an arranger; we weren't thinking about arrangements then. The band's style was built around Holder's and Fats Wall's improvisations. Fats had a style on alto different from any I had heard. Whatever he played, it was always swinging. And he had so many ideas! When he played a chorus I thought was exceptionally good, I would write it down and add the harmony for the other two saxophones, and add it to the stock arrangement. That way we could use it every night in a broader way than just a solo chorus. For the jitney dances we played – a nickel a dance and clear the floor – we used an introduction and two choruses of a tune, then an encore. The encore was the same tune with a slightly different sound. We used a modulation for the introduction, then went into a special chorus, or featured a solo, then out. Each dance set lasted about three minutes. But within the context of those times Holder's band was a swinging group.

We were also soon signed for a "live" half-hour noontime radio show sponsored by a local retail store. As Mangel's Melodians, we helped to push housewares, dry goods, shoes, and furniture for Mangel's Department Store. As far as I know, we were the first, or at least one of the first, bands used this way. A few years later the air waves were full of bands promoting everything from cigarettes to hair tonics.

We were into the fall and winter season after Holder signed a contract with the Northeast Amusement Company, owned by William Falkenburg and Andy Anderson. They were dance-hall promoters who operated park pavilions and dance halls in Tulsa and Oklahoma City 12 months of the year. That sounded like stability. We packed up and moved out of Holder's wife's house on Boll Avenue where we'd been living and rehearsing, sent for our wives, and settled down in Tulsa.

For the next two or three years our traveling consisted mainly of shuttling from Crystal City Park and the Louvre Ballroom in Tulsa to the Winter Garden and Spring Lake Park in Oklahoma City.

Our first season at the Winter Garden I was in for a real musical surprise. In came Jack Teagarden, with his trombone and baritone horn and seven-piece band, to play opposite us for one night as a special attraction. I want to say here that any time people saw a colored band they immediately expected it to play jazz and jazz only. And by the same token, white bands were expected to play "pretty" in conventional styles à la Guy Lombardo. Incidentally, we used to tune in on the radio to Lombardo and his Royal Canadians from Chicago. It was something different. One of the wives thought his name was divided a bit differently. Just before time for his broadcast, she'd say, "Oh, let's listen to Guylom Bardo," and whoever had the crystal set would tune him in and we'd all gather around. Another band we tuned in was Coon–Sanders – "the old left-hander" – out of Kansas City.

Anyway, at the Winter Garden that night Jack Teagarden, with his great jazz feeling, beat, and improvising, demolished the old stereotype of colored bands having a monopoly on jazz and Whites on sweet music. Here was a white band playing real New Orleans jazz. And I'll *never* forget one Teagarden-style waltz. The way he played *Let me call you sweetheart* it came out the jazziest, swingin'est waltz I ever heard. It was the only waltz he played that evening. We had to play the waltzes from then on. We played more white than Jack's band. And even though we were basically a swinging group, Teagarden was the real jazz attraction that night. And I picked up some good moving-bass ideas from his tuba player.

With our four steady locations, we could rehearse regularly and build up our book. Many of the tunes we played were head arrangements. By putting our talents and ideas together at rehearsals, we developed a style that dancers liked to dance to and listen to. We were pulling in crowds and pleasing our bookers, and we soon became Northeast's no.1 band.

Then in December 1928 came a blow. It was a Sunday morning and I'd gone out to get a paper. The headlines caught my eye. Something about an airplane accident on December 1st. I didn't read the story till I got home. Then Mary and I both got the shock of our lives. Four men, the story said, had been killed in that crash. One of them was my cousin Jimmy. I was heartbroken.

Jimmy had become a sort of mechanic, and before that, of course, he'd gotten to know a lot of wealthy people in Denver from working in their clubs. One of his rich friends, a man named Ballinger, owned a plane and was planning to set up his own airline service between Denver and San Antonio. He was going to take Jimmy on as his mechanic. They had flown to San Antonio and were on their way back to Denver. They had been warned of a snowstorm over the Texas Panhandle, but they had decided to risk getting through. They crashed in the storm. All four in the plane were burned beyond recognition.

I left for Denver immediately. While I was gone, Falkenberg gave Holder my pay to keep for me, but he never gave it to me. From then on Falkenberg was through with him. When Holder left the band on account of family problems, Falkenberg wanted me to be leader. "You've been conducting rehearsals," he said, "doing the arrangements, and you've had more experience than the others."

I wasn't too enthusiastic about the idea and did everything possible to get Holder back. He did return, but Falkenberg let me know he thought I was foolish to put up with this guy. But I knew Holder didn't mean to steal the money. He was trying to get his wife back and needed every cent. "Fellows, I'll try to do better," he kept reassuring us. I wouldn't fall out with him. What was a couple of bucks? I looked on him as a good trumpet player and leader.

But he soon left again, this time for good. The matter of succession came up again. Fats thought he should be leader because of all he'd contributed to the band with his original improvisations and creative ideas. He might have had other reasons, too, but he never brought them up to me. The band held an election, and I received the majority vote. Fats and I remained friends, though he left to form his own band. Theodore Ross, our third alto man, and Flip Benson, a trombone player, also left.

I sent to Denver for John Harrington, a Morrison alumnus, to come in on sax and clarinet. Someone recommended John Williams of Memphis and he came in on alto and baritone sax. We got Allen Durham, Eddie Durham's cousin, to replace Benson on trombone. Gene Prince took Holder's place on trumpet; he was well trained, a fine player. He later became an electronics expert on Long Island. With these replacements we still had a good band and Falkenberg was still pleased with the sound.

Northeast was expanding its territory, adding more ballrooms – one in Drumright, Oklahoma, and the Bluebird in Shawnee. So Northeast sent an efficiency expert from Detroit to Tulsa to manage the pavilion in Crystal City Park where we were playing, and to do a little public relations groundwork for what looked like our expanded travel schedule. You see, all the other bands on Northeast's circuit were white. In no time, the efficiency expert had a solution for averting booking confusions that might set off incidents. We would be called Andy Kirk and his Dark Clouds of Joy. One of the first things I did as a leader was drop the "dark" from the Clouds. I'd heard that expression back in Denver. It usually came from men hanging around in front of a saloon with nothing to do. When some of us came down the street towards them they'd remark, "Looks like it's gonna rain. Dark clouds comin'." I'd turn my back to them and look up at the sky, see if I saw any clouds.

We became Andy Kirk and his Twelve Clouds of Joy.

We were doing such good business for Northeast that the company decided it wanted another Andy Kirk on its roster. The choice was George E. Lee of Kansas City. On their way to Spring Lake Park in Oklahoma City, George and the band stopped in Tulsa to see us. I introduced them to the crowd and had them do some numbers at intermission. Like our band, Lee's was an entertaining band and had great variety. George himself played sax; his sister Julia played piano and sang with the band. They had a great brother-sister act – both of them sang; they could sing pop tunes, ballads, blues – everything – together and separately, and always went over big.

Later that evening George said to me, "By the way, Cab Calloway is breaking it up at El Torreon Ballroom in Kansas City. That's the Pla-Mor's rival." At that point those ballroom names meant nothing to me, so I just said, "Oh," and he went on, "The Pla-Mor's manager, Bennett Stydham, is looking for an out-of-town band to give Cab some competition. He doesn't want us. He wants new faces. Why don't you give him a call? No, better still, I'll call him myself."

The next night Stydham drove the 360-odd miles from Kansas City to Tulsa to hear us. In a day or two we had our contract. Thanks to George E. Lee, the Pla-Mor was about to have new faces. We didn't even know what a plum we'd picked off the 1929 Boom Tree when we rolled into Kansas City on that hot June day, the first out-of-town colored band to play the Pla-Mor. We were replacing Chick Scoggins, the Pla-Mor's white house band.

On the way we had stopped over in Topeka to play a one-nighter at a club called the Old Mill. Mary had decided to come directly to Kansas City later by train, so at the suggestion of a friend I stayed at the home of Mr and Mrs John Barker. Mr Barker was a letter carrier. We started right in talking shop. My stay at the Barker home was the beginning of a friendship between our families that lasted all through the years.

This music-making, I was to learn, wasn't just business and business relationships, but the means of forming close personal friendships with the people we played for and stayed with all across the country.

Mrs Barker was not only hospitable, she was a wonderful cook. She fed the whole band that night before the job. The next morning I told her I didn't know a thing about Kansas City and was kind of wondering where Mary and I would live. "That's no problem," she said. "Our daughter Eva and her husband live in Kansas City. They'd love to put you up. They've got three-year-old twins, but you won't mind, they're so cute. I'll call her, tell her to expect you."

As time went on, not only did we come to know Eva and her family; we met one of the Barkers' sons, who owned a grocery store in Topeka, and Eva's sister Theresa, who eventually taught at City College in New York. Today three of the Barker daughters are retired and live in the old family home on Western Avenue, the very house I stayed in that night in June 1929.

We went into the Pla-Mor at 32nd and Main that first night excited, a little nervous, but ready to give Cab at the El Torreon a real battle. There was just one hitch. We got the news that Cab had already left. We were alone on the battlefield. We went into our theme, *You can take it from me*, with feeling.

Stydham came up on the stand and introduced us to the dancers: "Ladies and gentlemen, this is Andy Kirk and his Twelve Clouds of Joy. We brought them in from Oklahoma where everybody loves them. We know you'll love them, too. Let's welcome Andy Kirk and the band!" They did. And every Cloud's face that I could see from behind my sousaphone had a big grin.

I want to explain why I wasn't up front leading the band. In those days a band's name was more important than the leader's name. At El Torreon Cab Calloway had fronted a band called the Missourians. It was not Cab Calloway and his Orchestra, that later became famous. One of Northeast's well-known white bands was called the Gloom Chasers, but in all the time we worked for Northeast I never knew who Mr Gloom was. And we were known by our name, Clouds of Joy, far more than by Andy Kirk. So I was playing sousaphone in the band and Billy Massey was fronting it.

People were dance crazy in those days. And if you played the kind of music they liked to dance to, that's what mattered. As I've said, our band didn't stress jazz, though we played it. We emphasized dance music – romantic ballads and pop tunes and waltzes – Viennese as well as standard popular waltzes like *Kiss me again* and *Alice Blue Gown*. I loved to play waltzes. We were first and last a dance orchestra, because people were dancing. I was "brought up" in the dance music field, and that influenced me.

We were also great on entertainment. We put on a ten-minute show every night with loud, fast stuff and it used to break everybody up. One of our big entertainment numbers was the novelty *Casey Jones*. We dressed up in engineers' black caps and tied red bandanas around our necks. Just before going into our routine I would borrow a cigarette from one of the smokers – I didn't smoke myself – take the mouthpiece off the sousaphone and blow a lot of smoke into the tubing. Massey sang the verse, then the whole band would come in on "Casey Jones, mounted to the cabin, Casey Jones, with the throttle in his hand . . . " By the time I got out front, smoke was pouring out of the bell of my horn. Allen Durham was imitating the drive shaft of a train engine with his trombone, and Big Jim Lawson was dancing a jig as he "oiled" the "drive shaft" with his trumpet.

The crowds loved it, especially white audiences. They'd gather around the bandstand and clap and yell, "Let's get hot. Come on, get hot." Whites used expressions like that to egg us on.

Only Whites could come to dance and attend sports events at the Pla-Mor, which was a regular entertainment complex with an arena for hockey besides the ballroom. The Clouds always got passes to the hockey games. We were the only Blacks in the audience, of course, and we got plenty of stares and looks until word was passed around that it was OK, we were the band. Then everybody forgot all about us and watched the game.

That first summer in Kansas City started us on a whole new way of life. In ways that might seem unimportant now, but they were all part of the Clouds – and the Kirks – moving up. One of those seemingly unimportant things was uniforms for the band. We never thought about it in Oklahoma. There we wore tuxes in winter, summer suits in summer. But our second night at the Pla-Mor Stydham said, "You've got a good-looking bunch of boys. Let's dress them up." Dressing up meant, first of all, looking cool – and being cool, if possible. Kansas City, we found out, was one hot place in summer. Mary used to get disgusted with me for going out to play baseball in those torrid temperatures. "Where are you going in all this heat?" she'd ask.

"Oh, I've got to go down and see about some business," I'd say. I didn't always let her know exactly where I was going.

For cooling the ballroom in those pre-air-conditioning days we had to depend on fans. They were the ceiling type with those great big blades that looked like airplane propellers. To reinforce the illusion of deep cool we had one uniform of white pants, white shoes, white shirts and white sleeveless sweaters. Then for one change we wore suits of light tan tweed with a brown dot, white shirts and brown ties. For another change we went into the current sports look – plus-fours! They were *the* fashion on every golf course. With our plus-fours we wore open-collar white shirts and our sleeveless sweaters. And did we look sharp! For formal affairs we wore tuxes.

Our tailor was J. B. Simpson of Chicago, but we bought all our ties and socks and other accessories at Matlaw's on the southeast corner of 18th and Vine. It's still in business on that same corner.

Dressing up wasn't all that Stydham did for us. I'll get to that but first I have to backtrack a bit and talk about our union status. For the first time we could all belong to the same local of the musicians' union. Up till this time we had all belonged to various segregated locals. But we resigned from them and joined local 627, the Kansas City black local. We became officially known as a Kansas City orchestra, though we were still a territory band.

When we had a traveling band status, whenever we played a white ballroom or club in a town, the white local had jurisdiction and we had to deposit our contract with that local. This was the case when T. Holder had the band at the Ozarks Club near Dallas. We deposited our contract with the white local in Dallas. Even though it was the South, we had no trouble with the Dallas local. Its officers treated us like men. The Oklahoma City local was never a problem, either.

Tulsa was a different matter. At that time the State of Oklahoma had segregation laws that prevented us from belonging to the all-white musicians' local 94 in Tulsa. Although we had lived and worked in that jurisdiction for over three years, we remained under the traveling band status. That meant any contract we filed must show 10 percent above existing local scale, according to the laws of the AFM (American Federation of Musicians). This we always did, and that local always accepted our contract without question.

But naturally the members of the Tulsa local wanted to play the best spot – which we had – but each time we deposited our contract with the white local there it was accepted. Falkenberg gave us a raise each time, too, so we would as a consequence be over scale. But we learned later that Daddy Fox, the local's secretary, kept asking Falkenberg, "Why do you keep using this band?" It was a natural question. He was trying to take care of his own members. Falkenberg had told us that Fox was after him to put in a local band and that his answer always was, "OK, give us one that'll do as well as these boys." Apparently he never could find a local white band that was good enough.

Before our last engagement at Crystal City Park, and our departure for Kansas City, Fox tried some dirty tricks. Unbeknown to us or to Falkenberg, he raised the scale for the engagement. We deposited our contract as usual, but after we got to the Pla-Mor the federation notified Stydham that we had violated the law by working under scale in Tulsa. They slapped an $1800 fine on us. That had been Fox's ploy to get us out.

I was very upset, but Stydham said, "Don't worry, you're doing fine business for us. We'll pay the fine."

Fox's dirty tricks reflected the southern thinking of the time, and the federation couldn't have cared less, either. It made no attempts to get the facts, just went along with Daddy Fox's claim. Nothing like that would or could happen today. If you bring in a contract below the scale you're notified what scale is, and it is not accepted.

Local 627 in Kansas City had its own building, so we always had a place to rehearse if we needed it. It was a place all the musicians could meet together, do a little jamming upstairs. At one point, though, there was trouble between the black and white locals in Kansas City. So Petrillo, then AFM president, sent one of his right-hand men, Ray Jackson – a black man – down to look into it. Of course it was black bands that made Kansas City's reputation as a jazz city. The white union didn't have any rehearsed orchestras, so Blacks got all the jobs. White kids wanted to join the black local. No wonder! The array of Kansas City black bands in the pre-Depression and Depression years constituted a Hall of Fame all its own: Bennie Moten, George E. Lee, Paul Banks, Clarence Love, Thaymon Hayes, Harlan Leonard. And there was Jap Allen, a young band that at one time included Ben Webster and Clyde Hart.

Up until 1973 Local 627 was still 627, not merged with white Local 34. Since merging it has become known as Local 34–627, but to retain its values and identity 627 became the Musicians' Foundation. Now all business is done in 34–627, but the property, consisting of the two-storey building, is still under the Musicians' Foundation. There's a museum in the building with a history of Kansas City in its archives, and pictures of all the famous Kansas City bands – those I've mentioned plus Count Basie, Jay McShann, Walter Page and the Blue Devils, our band, and others.

As our popularity grew we played both white ballrooms, the Pla-Mor and the El Torreon, and other spots. One was an exclusive white club called the Vanity Fair, a nightclub owned by the Lusco brothers a few doors from Jenkins' Music Store on Walnut Street. Another of our white locations was a roadhouse out by the dog track in North Kansas City. It was run by Johnny Lazzia, the man who protected Pretty Boy Floyd. Harry Truman was then a county judge. We were popular with all those white audiences. In fact, we were often thought of as a white band because of our smooth style and our emphasis on ballads and waltzes.

But – and this is important – we were also playing our share of black dances, along with the native Kansas City black bands, at the two black ballrooms – Labor Temple and "15th and Paseo." The latter, known formally as the Dancing Academy, took its popular name from its location at 15th and Paseo, and it was universally known by that name.

Even though our band didn't play in any of the little jazz clubs – they weren't our size or style – most of the boys beelined it to them every night after our job at the Pla-Mor. Quitting time was 12:30 a.m., and I usually had something to say about rehearsals or new routines, but by the time I got my horn packed up, half of the band would be gone.

There were good music kicks right at the Pla-Mor, when bands like McKinney's Cotton Pickers or Fletcher Henderson shared the stand with us. The Cotton Pickers played something I'd never heard before; a sixth in a chord. In some places it sounded to me like a clash. I was used to triads, dominant sevenths, a dominant ninth occasionally, and diminished chords. Later I got to like the sound of the sixth, especially the way Don Redman used it in his arrangements, as a 13th an octave higher. I heard lots of Don's arranging ideas years later when we both lived here at 555 Edgecombe. He didn't have a piano so he'd ring our bell. "Could I use your piano a minute? I want to try a few chords."

"OK. Sure."

"Thanks."

He did all his arranging without a piano of his own, but ours was available when he had to hear an idea a little more forcefully.

At the Pla-Mor Fletcher Henderson was the band that really opened our ears. When they came in to guest for a night, the Clouds of Joy stood around the bandstand just like the customers, soaking up the sound. Their 16 pieces, of course, delivered a bigger sound than our 12, but it wasn't just numbers that made the impact. Their beat was different from ours. They had a two-beat drive, powerhouse all the time. We played four-beat, a little bounce-beat style. They had what we called the eastern sound and they did a lot of show tunes. That was natural for a New York band.

Fletcher and I became good friends. Our bands were different, but there were certain things he liked about the Clouds of Joy. To prove it, he made an arrangement of a Broadway show tune especially for us. Later he recommended me as his replacement at the Roseland Ballroom in New York. A couple of years after that we actually metamorphosed for a night into Fletcher Henderson and his Orchestra. He'd had some sort of mix-up in his bookings and couldn't make a date – a very important debutante party at a big hotel in Cincinnati. We were in the area so he got us to pinch-hit for him, and at double what we'd been getting. He did put in an appearance himself during the evening, and played a few numbers on piano. Apparently no one suspected it wasn't his band, except one guy who came up to him and smiled and said, "You're about the fastest man I've ever seen. I listened to your band on the radio from New York just half an hour ago, and now here you are entertaining us in Cincinnati."

5

The first big date in New York

Another Sunday. It was nearly a year since we'd started meeting over Andy's story in the study at 14-B and stoking up afterwards on Mary's and her sister Bernice's five-star dinners. Kansas City excited Andy, but not in quite the same way it did the jazz addicts.

Oh, I heard all the little jazz groups from time to time, but not as a regular diet. I went home to be with Mary. We were expecting our first child. That to me was more exciting than all the blues and jazz in Kansas City.

We had begun to feel at home in Kansas City and had already developed a warm friendship with the Barkers' daughter Eva and her family. We were still living with them when little Andy was born. Mary's brother, Jimmy Colston, and I walked the floor there for hours while Mary was giving birth. Jimmy and his wife Natalie had moved to Kansas City before we did. Natalie was in charge of the baby ward at Phyllis Wheatley Hospital, where little Andy was born. She saw to it that everything new for babies he got.

After we left Eva's we moved to 1212 Woodland. That's when I heard a lot of Joe Turner, the famous blues shouter. He was working at Piney Brown's right around the corner on 12th Street. Piney ran the club for Felix Payne, a politician, who owned it. Turner and boogie-woogie pianist Pete Johnson kept rolling out blues till four and five in the morning. I didn't have to go to the club. It came to me through the windows. Sometimes I'd get disgusted: all that blues shouting and boogie-woogie kept me awake.

But all kinds of great things were happening for us. The band was going over big wherever we played. And Mary and I were experiencing a whole new social life. That's another reason I wasn't hanging out in the jazz clubs. We were meeting a lot of people – Blacks in the school system, in business, in the professions. It was a revelation to me. Kansas City was a regular mecca for young Blacks from other parts of the country aspiring to higher things than janitor or chauffeur.

The City had three hospitals, General I and II, and Phyllis Wheatley. Blacks planning careers in medicine interned at General II and nurses took their training there. One of the young interns we met was Dr Theodore Pinckney, who later became a well-known physician in Washington DC, and we are still friends to this day. Another prominent Washington physician, Dr Sparky Adams, who had been an athlete at West Virginia State, also interned in Kansas City. I stayed at his home in Washington when I contracted pneumonia during an engagement we played at the Howard Theater.

Not all the bright young interns went to Washington. Dr Maddox, Mary's baby doctor, continued his practice in Indianapolis. Mrs Eva Thomas, Tommy to us, a top nurse at General II, subsequently came to New York to join the staff at Harlem Hospital, known then as Memorial Hospital. When I was managing the Theresa Hotel in Harlem she had an apartment there. She didn't believe in drugs, she'd seen so much in her career as a nurse.

Mary had joined several social clubs and was involved with their activities. Social clubs were the negro way of life. Kansas City was a very segregated city, but as far as I could see Blacks didn't care. They had their own theaters and all types of black entertainment, their own clubs, ballrooms, bars and grills, their own homes in residential areas, and their own newspaper, the *Kansas City Call*. That paper was a training ground for young black newspapermen. Roy and Earl Wilkins were on the *Call*. I knew Roy on close speaking terms.

In short, Blacks in Kansas city had their own everything, even their own baseball team, the Monarchs. Satchel Paige was then pitching for the Monarchs and was already an old man, in baseball terminology, when he came to the New York Yankees. Sundays everybody would be in Muelebach Park to see Monarch games. They drew Whites, too. The fact that Babe Ruth with the American All Stars and later Dizzy and Daffy Dean with the National All Stars came to play the Monarchs in post-season games told something about the caliber of the team.

That Kansas City Blacks, in my opinion, didn't care about being restricted to their own segregated social life was indicated to me in the Civil Rights movement of the 1960s. Most public places had been opened to Blacks, though I think a lot of white owners were afraid, at first, that their clubs and restaurants would be overrun with them. On a visit we made to Kansas City in the 1960s, four of us went to Pucci's, an exclusive restaurant in the country-club section. We ran into just one other colored person there, a woman dining alone. The rush to the white world was not on. Black reasoning could be summed up: "If you ain't got no pig's knuckles, why should we come here?"

But back in 1929 we experienced another Kansas City phenomenon. Everybody who lived through it knows about 24 October 1929, the day the stock market hit bottom. The Crash. Fortunes, careers, lives wiped out in an instant. In Kansas City it was like a pin dropping; the blast of jazz and blues drowned it out. People were crowding the clubs and ballrooms as usual. In other cities rich men, suddenly penniless, were committing suicide.

Evidently it was the political set-up under Pendergast that kept everything moving in Kansas City. I don't know, I'm not a politician. But good fortune continued to dog us. Recording executives Jack Kapp and Dick Voynow came down from Chicago looking for race artists for the Brunswick and Vocalion labels. Okeh had been in the race field since 1923, so it had a six-year jump on them. I didn't know then that was the purpose of their search. I thought they were just looking for new talent. They auditioned us at the Pla-Mor and four other bands at other spots.

That audition turned out to be a real "sleeper." We were all set up and ready except for Marion Jackson, our pianist. Nobody seemed to know where he was. Things were getting tense. We'd have to start soon or blow it. John Williams said,

"How about getting Prelude?" Prelude was our name for his wife, Mary Lou. When John first came on the band he had asked me to hear her play. I did and agreed with him that she was a fine pianist, but we already had one that met our requirements. And we were making a lot of road trips and I always thought doing one-nighters would be hard on a woman. But this was an emergency. I told John, OK. When Mary Lou came in and sat down at the piano to audition with us, no one had the wildest idea she'd be a big factor in our landing an excellent two-year recording contract, or, wilder yet, that she would make jazz history.

We had our first recording session on 7 November 1929 at the Kansas radio station KMBC. We recorded a couple of the original things John and Mary Lou brought to the audition – *Mess-a-Stomp* and *Blue Clarinet Stomp*. Mary Lou was on the recording date because she'd done the audition with us, and Kapp and Voynow didn't know that she wasn't our regular pianist. The other tune we did was *Casey Jones*. We had another recording session on 11 November, where we did Mary Lou's *Froggy Bottom*. Froggy bottom was literally along river banks. Figuratively it was in "the bottoms," the low part of town where many Blacks had little barbecue places. In some cites there were little clubs named Froggy Bottom for the tune. Blacks doing menial jobs were used to "the bottoms."

Remember, Moten had been *the* band on Okeh. What he was doing was what Brunswick and Vocalion wanted us to do. So we continued to do a lot of that – things like *Snag It*, *Mary's Idea*, and *Dallas Blues*. That type of number was the smaller part of our library. The bigger part we could play only in person.

We came east in January 1930 for our first date in New York. It was at the Roseland Ballroom, the one Fletcher Henderson had recommended us for. Because of floods in Ohio we had to travel via Memphis, Tennessee. It was a very roundabout way and we ran short of money. After we got in I went straight to the Roseland and explained to Brecker, the manager, what had happened and that we needed money.

He stared coldly at me and said, "You've got some nerve! I don't know whether I'm going to keep you or not."

That chilly welcome was my first clue that New York was different from the rest of the country. Now I'm beginning to see this is the eastern-strictly-business approach. In western style a man's word was his bond; agreements were sealed with a handshake. But Brecker did give us an advance, and kept us on.

Here it was – the Clouds' first big date in New York! The Roseland was an important spot for bands. Yet Andy passed over it as though it was a one-nighter in Sioux Falls, North Dakota. Wasn't it exciting being at the Roseland in New York? He shrugged off questions about it in his typical self-effacing way. It was, of course, another ballroom in a lengthening succession of ballrooms long since called home by the Clouds of Joy. Did the city or town really matter that much?

Oh, I don't know. It was all right, I guess. We were there for six weeks. Opposite us on the other bandstand was Milt Shaw for two weeks, Casa Loma for two weeks, and Freddy Bergen for two weeks. In April we traveled to Chicago for another recording date. Along the the way we played places like Columbia and Hannibal, Missouri, and La Salle, Illinois.

When Kapp and Voynow came into the recording studio in the Furniture Mart Building in Chicago where we were set up, they looked over towards the piano, saw Jack (Marion Jackson), and said, "Where's the girl? We liked her style." We sent for Mary Lou that time, and later she did more recording dates with us before she joined the band as regular pianist in 1931. And from then on she was a tremendous influence on our music and a star attraction in the band.

Recordings in the 1930s were made on wax. There'd be A, B, and C wax. On our Chicago sessions the A & R man supervising the date would at some point say, "All right, let's do some with the girl and the rhythm section." They'd make a master pressing – the A wax. It would eventually wear out, then they'd have to go to the B or C wax. Mary Lou would of course be improvising on all three. So when the B or C sides came out people who bought them would say, "That doesn't sound the way she did before."

Of course not. Her ideas were new all the time.

From the start she wanted to write arrangements. She would have certain chords in her mind but she didn't at first know how to voice them. She had a good ear and tried to write down what she heard. If she wasn't out all night at the jazz clubs in Kansas City, listening and getting ideas, she'd be sitting up at the foot of the bed, legs crossed like an Indian, just writing and writing, while John was sleeping. Sometimes she'd stay up all night working at her arrangements. She'd try one thing, then another, get mad, and start over. As time went on she learned voicing for the different horns from things I showed her from some arrangements I'd bought.

I'd been fortunate enough to pick up 40 professional arrangements from Hank Biagini, who had led the Casa Loma band when it was a Goldkette unit called the Orange Blossoms, but had pulled out of Casa Loma when we played opposite them at the Roseland. Some were by Don Redman, some by Gene Gifford. We sounded like a new band. We played at 15th and Paseo with this different sound.

Mary Lou and I collaborated on one race thing we recorded. She wrote the first part in minor, I finished it in major. I called it *Corky* after Skeezix's brother who had just been born in the "Gasoline Alley" comic strip.

All the time we were making race records we were playing our pop tunes, romantic ballads, and waltzes for the dancing public. Most of our work in ballrooms was for Whites, and these were the things they liked to dance to. Our arrangements did allow for solo improvisations and other improvised parts, though. But the people who controlled the output and distribution for Brunswick and Vocalion never gave a thought to that side of our band, or the market we played for in white ballrooms. In fact, they had a black man, Mayo Williams, in Chicago to handle race records, channeling them to the race market. Maybe they thought Whites wouldn't want race records, and that Andy Kirk and the

Clouds of Joy couldn't make any other kind. It was all part of the racial setup and climate of the times.

Not only record companies turned deaf ears. Most white publishers didn't want black "trash," either. Ears were attuned to European music. Those who controlled the business didn't seem to consider that we had an American music.

If we weren't on location in Kansas City, we'd go out on one-nighters, following those spokes into known and unknown territory. Playing one-nighters in those Depression years of the early 1930s was all part of making a living in music. We didn't have to depend on one location. Most of the one-nighters we played were ballrooms with names like Dreamland, Rainbow, Ritz, Cinderella. They reflected the euphoria left over from World War I. We had fought to make the world safe for democracy. There would never be any more war, and, even though we had a Depression, Americans had always overcome everything. So as long as there wouldn't be another war, we could get out of the Depression.

In my hometown of Denver we sometimes played the Rainbow Ballroom for two or three weeks. White patronage, except Mondays, when Blacks rented it. In Greeley, Colorado, we played for a ballroom owner named Norcross. He had to stage special come-ons – in cherry-picking time it was "Cherry Pie Day" – to lure enough customers to stay in business. We had to get out of Kansas City to find out there was a Depression.

Bookings mushroomed by a kind of grapevine system. Ballroom owners would tell each other about bands they were currently featuring, and, as word was passed along, the bands followed. One of the main circuits we played was managed by Tom Archer. He owned a ballroom in Omaha, Nebraska, and another, the Arkota, in Sioux Falls, South Dakota.

By the way, early in 1976 a young guy came in to the Local 802 office here in New York, where I worked, to make out an application for the union. I noticed he was from Sioux Falls. I asked him if the Arkota Ballroom was still there. "Believe it or not," he said, "it is."

"I used to work there," I said.

If we were in Omaha, it was a pretty sure bet we would play the whole Archer circuit – cities like Des Moines, Mason City, Cedar Rapids, Dodge City, Waterloo, St Jo, Sioux Falls. There were at least five we could always count on. Sometimes we played dates at smaller places, even getting up into Minnesota. That was great polka country. Whenever we were finishing a date I would always announce the next attraction. More than once it was Lawrence Welk. Then he was playing the squeeze box and leading a six- or eight-piece band. All the bands on the Archer circuit were white except George E. Lee's and the Clouds of Joy.

In Faribault, Minnesota, Mary and I stayed at a little hotel owned by a frugal yet service-minded man. He came to our door every morning at eight o'clock to get the sheets from our bed to wash them so we could have clean sheets that night. In spite of the forced early rising, we enjoyed our stay there. No prejudice at all.

One time we played a dance in a little town in Iowa – Weldon, south of Des Moines – where, again, there were no colored folks. The morning we arrived we checked into the one little hotel in town, no trouble. Mary and I had little Andy with us. He was about three and so cute he attracted attention everywhere. We found out from the owner, who was soon calling Mary "Little Mother," that the town wanted to get lights for the ball field so they could have night games. That afternoon the Clouds' softball team took on the town team, and passed the hat for the cause. That night the whole town came to the dance.

Next morning some kids stopped by on their way to school and asked if they could take little Andy with them. They'd never seen a little colored kid before. So while he was being showed around – and showed off – at school, we all got out our bats and gloves and took on the town team again.

We had a regular athletic tournament, with foot races and other events. Mary and I both entered the races. Athletics were outlets for us on the road. Helped us get the kinks out after driving miles and miles cramped up with our instruments, baggage, bats and balls, and boxing gloves. Most of the time we traveled in cars, and we tried to plan our schedule – especially when we were doing territory work around Oklahoma – to stop about 7:00 p.m. at a gas station where there was a radio so we could hear "Amos 'n' Andy." This was a must. We liked their humor. The characters they played reminded us of people we knew in real life.

If we weren't driving our cars, we rented a bus with a driver, like a school bus. One driver we called the "Timid Soul." We stopped for an oil change in Indianapolis. The service-station man had him back the bus into the garage and the bus was so high the top of it scraped the garage door and ceiling. This called for strong words, but Timid Soul never used profanity, so he sputtered, "You . . . you . . . horse's neck!"

We played all across the state of Pennsylvania – Pittsburgh, Uniontown, Latrobe, Johnstown, Altoona, State College, Gettysburg. Pennsylvania was a great dance state, Ohio, too. There seemed to be more dance halls in those states than in most others. But there weren't facilities and sleeping accomodations for us in most towns as there were for the white bands. So we'd make our headquarters around Pittsburgh and fan out from there into Latrobe, Johnstown, and Youngstown, Ohio. We could stay in Youngstown. There was a colored hotel and colored Y's. And we could stay in Altoona. From there we might go to Harrisburg and work two or three dates out there. Harrisburg had a colored hotel. We could even stay in Pottsville at a rooming house. The lady who ran it even cooked for us. If I had Mary with me, we'd always find a room in a private home.

On one of our dates we were afloat. We played on a barge, Reese's Houseboat, on the Susquehanna River. We'd start at eight o'clock in the evening, move out into midstream, then return at 9:30. We played at the pier for 15 minutes before shoving off, and after coming to port while passengers came on and got off.

We didn't come into New York City on these Pennsylvania tours, but we might hit upstate cities like Utica and Syracuse after a one-nighter at Johnson City. One jump from Syracuse to Pottsville I remember because I didn't make it. I had a touch of pneumonia and had to stay behind to recover. When we did come into New York, it was just to play the Savoy Ballroom. We were still classified as a territory band and we had no big records out, just the race records that reached only Blacks. But we were playing more and more college dates – white and black – and naturally we played music the college kids liked to dance to. The record companies *still* didn't know what our band was like.

The first time the Depression really came home to us was in Arkansas, when we ran into the bank holiday from 6th to 9th March 1933. We had been working the Malco houses, a small theater chain in the state, and had started out with a good contract. But now, as we drove into each town, we'd get the word, "The theater's closed." Things were getting desperate so we stopped at the Malco home office in North Little Rock. "There's nothing we can do," they said. "This was unforeseen."

John Williams and I got our heads together and worked out a plan. "Tell you what," John said, "let's us go on to my house in Memphis and scout around there and see if there's any work." I had some gold coins paid us for a job we played in Fort Smith, Arkansas, on the Oklahoma border. So I left the gold pieces with the band, and John and I took off for Memphis. We had played a few times there at Fair Park for a Mr Bennett, who was manager of the ballroom in the park. I went out to see him. He was busy when I got there. I listened to the band for a while – it was Joe Sanders, "the old left-hander" – till I got a chance to talk to Bennett.

At intermission he announced, "Friends, I have good news. Our friend Andy Kirk is here, and he and his band will be in soon to play for us." Mr Bennett even gave me an advance to get the band over from Little Rock.

Next day I went to see Buster Bailey's sister, who was working at the Booker T. Washington School. She was able to set up a concert date for us at the school. We added another date, the Pink Rose Ballroom in Memphis, run by Robert Henry, where John and Mary Lou had had their own group before joining the Clouds of Joy. St Louis netted us a one-nighter, a dance at the Pullman Porters' Club. A date in Hannibal turned out to be a flop. Nobody came. There hadn't been enough time to publicize it. With money so short, people needed about a month to get primed for spending what little they had on any one dance. But with our Memphis and St Louis dates we made enough to get back to Kansas City. We came in on a Saturday night. The whole town was wide open, as usual. Clubs were going full blast, lights were bright. No bank holiday anywhere to be seen. And we had a job practically waiting for us. The union had told Vanity Fair that Andy Kirk was due in, and that meant work for us.

The Vanity Fair was like a private club. Those who came had to have a key to get in. The club served good meals and put on good shows. They were choreographed by Joe Stevens of Chicago. Chicago was almost shut down, so Joe brought down good acts from there. We had a chorus line of about ten girls, though the "line" was really a circle because the club had a revolving bandstand in the center of the room. Bea Ellis, the girl who became Duke Ellington's second wife, was in the line, and Johnny Hodges's future wife tagged the line. She was only about 16. We called her Skeezix. The dancers danced counter-clockwise to us as we moved slowly round and round on our revolving bandstand. It made for easy communication.

"Get your favorite request played," we'd tell the dancers, and they'd let us know what they wanted to hear.

We were the only black band to play the Vanity Fair, as I recall. During our engagement we got into a regular routine of bragging to the waiters about our ball-playing. The band belonged to a softball league in the city, besides playing other bands like McKinney's Cotton Pickers at Paseo Park. It came naturally to brag about how we could play ball. The waiters finally had heard enough. "Listen," they said, "we're tired hearing you talk about what a ball team you have. Now we're going to show *you* something about playing ball." They had gotten up a team. Jim Lusco, one of the club owners, was pitcher. We took up their challenge. At the end of the game they were nothing. We beat 'em, 30 to 3. Lusco may have known how to run a nightclub, but he didn't know how to put a spin on a ball. He just threw it and we'd knock it out of the park.

Besides our white dance jobs, the Clouds played their share of black society affairs at Labor Temple and 15th and Paseo. There were so many social clubs giving dances and parties – break-o-day dances, breakfast dances, matinee dances, grand balls – that all the bands worked all the time. Every group in Kansas City's segregated black society – teachers, nurses, doctors, school principals, politicians – had its club. We had social clubs in Denver, but nowhere near the number Kansas City had. Being such a small minority in Denver and having no segregated schools, we had not developed a professional elite. Teachers then were all white; so were school principals, doctors, lawyers, and nurses. Blacks were on the domestic level. It's different today. Denver has black teachers and other professional people.

Fraternal organizations like the Elks, Odd Fellows, Masons, and Knights of Pythias also flourished in Kansas City. Sometimes we played for their annual conventions. Many Blacks belonged to these organizations. They owned their own halls, and when they weren't using them they rented them to various local social clubs. These organizations all had a kind of religious tie-up, and a high point of their conventions was generally a sermon by some preacher. They ended, however, on a more secular note: banquet and dancing to the music of Andy Kirk and the Twelve Clouds of Joy.

Kansas City as a whole had a real appreciation for its adopted sons, the Clouds of Joy. We reached lots of people. Our music pleased both Blacks and Whites.

Of all the "native sons" bands, George E. Lee's was closest in style to mine because we were both entertaining bands and we stressed dance music. Being similar, we were more competitive with each other than with Moten and the bands in his groove. But we made a gentleman's agreement on a minimum price we'd never go below. We played several of the same places, and we never had any trouble.

Mary had a little band for a while, too. Charlie Parker was in it. That was when he was just starting out. Another time she got a group lined up for one of the small clubs, went down the first night to work and the manager said, "Now I'm sorry we can't pay you anything in money, but we'll give you your dinner."

Mary said, "I'm not that hungry. I eat at home."

6

Until the real thing comes along

Fall was again sharpening the air. Lamps came on earlier. In the study at 14-B Andy talked as calmly as ever, yet there was a feeling of something major coming into focus.

The summer of 1934 the Clouds were signed to play at Winwood Beach Amusement Park outside Kansas City. The park itself was owned by a man named Glover. He also owned a business in the city, Glover Mange Cure, as I remember. The hill beyond the park was dotted with summer cabins. One was used by Glover and his wife and children. He moved them out there every summer for vacation. The man who leased the ballroom in the park was the one who hired us. He was a smart Jew. He told Glover he would need two cabins as part of his lease, one for himself and one for the bandleader. It was all settled that way before we moved out for the summer.

Glover's cabin, as it happened, was right across from ours. When he learned who was to be his new neighbor, he protested to the ballroom operator. "What can I do?" the operator said. "We've signed the contract." I went out before the season opened to clean up the property, do some weeding in the yard and garden around our cabin. I wanted it nice before we moved in. I had no tools so I went down to the commissary in the park and borrowed some from the caretaker. I went back to the cabin and started weeding.

Mrs Glover happened to be at her cabin that afternoon and saw me. She hadn't been living with black folks on the same level. Or altitude. She came over and said to me, "You can't use those garden tools. They're my private tools. You have no business with them."

"The caretaker loaned them to me," I explained.

"I don't care who loaned them to you," she said, "they're mine and you can't use them."

That was that, but I figured out some way to clean up the property so it was in order and neat when the job started and we moved in.

In a day or so, little Andy was out playing around and wandered over to the Glovers' cabin. He didn't know anything about segregation. Mary saw Mrs Glover talking to him and that he was welcome. When it was Mary's turn to entertain her card club, she invited the members out to our cabin for the day. They were all dressed up and everybody had a good time out there, where the air was clean and fresh. We got no complaints from the Glovers.

Mary could walk over a $10 bill. Her head was always in the air. One morning, soon after her club had been at the cabin, she and little Andy were walking to the commissary. Mrs Glover came along in her car, tooted the horn and offered them a lift. It was Mary's first conversation with Mrs Glover, and she asked right away if her club guests had in any way disturbed the Glovers. Mrs Glover assured her they had not.

One night I became ill and Mary was up with me all through the night. The next day Mrs Glover stopped her car by our cabin and said, "I saw the light on in your cabin all night. Was someone sick? Is there anything I can do?"

"Andy was sick," Mary said.

"You should have called me," she said. "I have a regular drugstore in our cabin. Is there anything I can do now?" Mary thanked her, said I was coming along fine and would be at work that night as usual. From then on there was a friendly feeling between us, but only little Andy went calling.

At the end of the summer, when we said our good-byes, Mrs Glover said, "We'd be happy to have you back."

That fall the band went into Billy Craig's Blossom Heath, a high-class white nightclub in Oklahoma City. Mary and little Andy stayed in Kansas City. Blossom Heath had a Columbia

Broadcasting wire which covered an area of maybe five states. That introduced us to new audiences in Arkansas, Oklahoma, Louisiana and Texas. Since they came to know us only by radio, they didn't know whether we were white or black.

After we returned to Kansas City and were playing at Fairyland Park, promoters who had picked up our broadcasts from Blossom Heath wrote to Harold Duncan, Fairyland's manager, to see if we were coming on tour. We signed a contract with Duncan to manage us, and he booked us on a tour of the Southwest. He had the guarantee – a certain amount of money – from the promoters. "What do you want to pay the men?" he asked me.

I suggested a figure I thought was fair, enough to cover extra expenses on tour, send some home to their wives, and give them a reasonable salary. "Ain't you afraid you'll spoil them?" he said.

Up until that moment I had had confidence in him. Now I was afraid of his thinking – that we weren't used to money and that a few dollars would spoil us. The implication was that the Clouds were not grown up, were not adults. The sum I had suggested I knew wouldn't spoil me, why should it spoil them? But he agreed, reluctantly, to the amount I had suggested, and we went on tour. I still liked him, but his question gave me an insight into his way of thinking. It didn't seem the best for a permanent business arrangement.

Back in Kansas City after the tour, I began to take stock of our situation. It was five years since we'd first signed a contract with Brunswick and Vocalion, in 1929, and we were still recording only race things. Yet we were pleasing both Blacks and Whites with our dance music in Kansas City and had by now traveled those spokes into many different territories. And I had Pha Terrell to sing the romantic ballads. He had joined us in 1933.

I first heard Pha in a little place run by an Italian on 18th Street and Charlotte, near Vine. Our trumpet man Irving "Mousie" Randolph was with me. When we came in Pha was singing *Lullaby of the Leaves* – and he swang it! He was also employed as the joint's manager and bouncer, in spite of his slight build and weight and his ability to sing in falsetto.

Mousie said, "I can't see him."

I'm glad I didn't agree with him. Pha turned out to be one of our band's biggest assets.

I decided it was time to try to crack the race barrier in recordings. I wrote to Brunswick and Vocalion in Chicago, told them we had some nice things to record. They had been taking just about anything we brought in for the race market. An answer came back that the office had been moved to New York, the company executives had been to London and gotten permission to use the Decca label, and if we came into New York, they'd be happy to record us.

George Crowe, a white kid who hung around all the bands in Kansas City, was about to play a significant part in this next step for the Clouds of Joy. Joe Glaser, Louis Armstrong's manager, had hired Crowe to go out with Louis as his road manager. By now Crowe was back in Kansas City and came to see us. I mentioned we were hoping to get into New York to record. He said, "I'll get in touch with Joe Glaser. He should be able to book you for some dates."

On Crowe's recommendation, Joe Glaser put us into the Astoria nightclub in Baltimore for two weeks, following Don Redman. He then arranged for us to play a dance for an organization in Philadelphia that needed a band. Louis Armstrong was in the city, too, at the Earle Theater. After his last show that night he came over to the dance and we were introduced to the crowd together.

From there we came into New York and went to the Decca studios. I asked Jack Kapp to listen to a ballad we wanted to record. Pha had been singing it, along with other ballads we featured.

"Andy, what's the matter with you?" Kapp said. "You've got something good going for you. Why do you want to do what the white boys are doing?" Right then I saw his commercial motives, saw why he had originally wanted to record us in Kansas City. It was for the race market only. He told us that for that session *Christopher Columbus* was a must.

Fletcher Henderson was already set with it on his label, but Joe Davis, who published it, was Kapp's brother-in-law and had asked Kapp to have me do it.

I knew Davis from earlier times. He had an office in the Roseland building, and when we played at the Roseland I used to hang out in his office because Alex Hill and Fats Waller were on his staff writing tunes. Alex Hill had played briefly in T. Holder's band, and I had met Fats Waller in Kansas City. Davis's ears were attuned to black music. He always liked what the Clouds were doing, and now, four or five years after first knowing each other, we were still friendly. We did *Christopher Columbus.*

"Great, fine," Kapp said, after hearing the playback. He gave me a pat on the back, one to Mary Lou, and all the rest of the band. "You did a wonderful job." He started for the door.

"Wait," I said, "you said you'd listen to our other things."

"Oh – OK," he said, "go ahead."

We played our special ballad. He said it was OK, but I could see it didn't really strike him. He had the race thing on his mind. But as a compromise he finally said, "All right, we'll record it." That ballad was a tune that came to life in Kansas City. Count Basie was playing at the Cherry Blossom between 18th and 19th streets on Vine, where entertainers from Chicago were featured. One was Harriet Calloway – no relation to Cab – who had been appearing in *Blackbirds.* The show wasn't a success, but there was one tune in it called *A Slave Song* that survived. Three kids with ukeleles hustled from one club to another singing and playing it and all the Kansas City bands picked it up. Harriet Calloway put words to it.

When we brought it to New York, hoping to record it – and we finally got an OK from Jack Kapp – he called Sammy Cahn and Saul Chapman, just kids themselves then, to write new lyrics. When it came out it had five writers' names on it. The three kids and their ukeleles got lost somewhere in the shuffle and have never been heard of since. Only after Cahn and Chapman wrote the new lyrics and we recorded it was the title changed to *Until the real thing comes along.*

We were back in Kansas City at Fairyland Park when *Real Thing* came out in the summer of 1936. We'd been playing it on our dates around town a lot, and it was a favorite with everyone, Black and White, so the recording came as no surprise there. Everybody already knew how it sounded when we played it.

One night Jesse Johnson, a black promoter from St Louis, stopped by to see if we'd play a date for him on a boat. He paid me what he owed me for dates we'd played at his little club in St Louis and left a deposit at the union for the boat job. It was to be the next Monday, our day off. We drove to St Louis, went down to the wharf to find the boat, and got a real shock when we saw the huge crowd milling around. It was big league ball-game size. They packed the boat to capacity and there were still a lot of people left behind on the wharf. We didn't know why all of a sudden we were a big favorite in St Louis. We hadn't attracted crowds like that at Jesse's club.

The boat moved out into the Mississippi. We played a set or two of some of our regular things, then went into *Real Thing*. People stopped dancing and rushed up to the bandstand and stood there listening. We played it seven times that evening before the boat docked at the wharf. We had to leave Kansas City to know we had a hit on our hands.

Back on the job at Fairyland, I got word from Mr Glover he wanted to see me. I went to his office. He said, "I've been reading about you and I'm happy for you. Be glad to have you back any time." How sweet it was!

When we returned for our next recording session I came in with some joogie things. One was *Git*. And what do you think Kapp said! "I'd like to have an arrangement on *Poor Butterfly*." *Poor Butterfly*! Shades of the employee elevator at Denver Dry Goods, where I sang and whistled it to my ups and downs!

So now – at last – we were into recording ballads as a result of *Real Thing* money coming in. We did two more, *What'll I tell my heart* and *Dedicated to you* along with *Lady who swings the band* and *Fifty-Second Street.* We did more ballads on another session: *Better Luck Next Time, I went to the gypsy, With love in my heart* and *Why can't we do it again.* I have to say, though, that I was sorry when Decca also cut down on our jazz.

Our ballads were selling. We jumped from 10,000 sales to 100,000. *Real Thing* was to widen our territory, open up new areas for jobs and help us to reach people of all levels. It was our real breakthrough from race records, and it became synonymous with Andy Kirk.

We stayed at Fairyland Park into September of 1936. The weather was good, and the rides were still going. Mary and our now school-age little Andy and I had moved into a furnished apartment in the Luther Dade Apartments, about the nicest apartment building the Blacks had. Joe Glaser came there to see me on his way to the coast. "Do nothing till I come back," he said. That was to keep me from accepting offers already pouring in. Several people were in Kansas City to make me propositions – John Hammond, Willard Alexander, and a club promoter from Chicago, among them. Mr Craig had called from Blossom Heath; people were asking him "When are you going to get the Clouds back?" Jimmy Buchanan called from New York about our coming into the Savoy.

Word came from Glaser: "Sending you air tickets on Braniff." I met him in Chicago on Labor Day – flew up and back – and we signed a contract. He bought our former contract with Duncan also. "Little Joe from Chicago" beat 'em all to the gun.

Glaser moved from Chicago to New York and rented space in the Rockwell-O'Keefe booking office. Duncan thought I was with Rockwell-O'Keefe and wrote to them that he had pictures of the band he'd like to get rid of and maybe they could use them. Later they gave me his letter. Duncan had also written: "By the way, how's my double-crossin' dinge?"

When I read that I thought, "Why, that little . . . " Then I said, "So what?" He was a little man, he thought little, but he didn't hold a grudge. A year or so later he invited me to his house.

I don't think I've ever been really angry. A little ruffled up sometimes, but I never lost my head in situations. The way I've looked at life all along was that if somebody said something once that didn't characterize him for life.

In 1937 we toured the South for the first time, riding the crest of *Real Thing*. You could hear it on jukeboxes. Those jukes were going all night in the South, especially in Florida. Territory bookers still dotted the landscape. There were two I remember in Florida – Bill Davies in Miami and Joe Higgins, who owned a music store in Jacksonville. Ralph Weinberg booked bands around the West Virginia area – Bluefield, Beckley, and Charleston – and over into North Carolina – Raleigh and Durham. In Houston, Texas, a booker named Don Roby owned the Peacock Ballroom and promoted dances. He had a night spot that featured a band with those great Texas tenormen Illinois Jacquet and Arnett Cobb, until Lionel Hampton came along and hired them away.

A dentist in Lake Charles, Louisiana, promoted dances as a sideline. Must have been a nice change from filling teeth all day. And there was Don Albert, a trumpet player – and a good one, too – who had a club in San Antonio. He was from New Orleans and could he cook! He'd tell The Hilltop, a white recreation place, about his bands and that way extend their San Antonio bookings. And of course there were Si Shribman and his brother Charlie, the well-known bookers in New England.

We toured the South extensively because that's where our records had sold best. We made friends among the fans, who always came to see us whenever we came their way. In Shreveport Dr Mye Haddock always brought his party to a table down front at the ballroom. And he was just one of many who supported us, north, south, east, and west.

From 1937 on we were doing about 50,000 miles a year. We had been using a fleet of Dodges at first. I burned out an axle in Port Arthur, Texas, called a wrecker, and then bought a Buick. It was a dream. I had it two years then bought another, a 1940 Buick – green, with white walls, and a radio, before radios were standard equipment. By then we were

Andy Kirk, c1920

Andy's wife, Mary

Mary Banion, Andy's aunt

Early Wheels: George Morrison's band in the hills of Colorado, June 1924; Andy is sixth from the right.

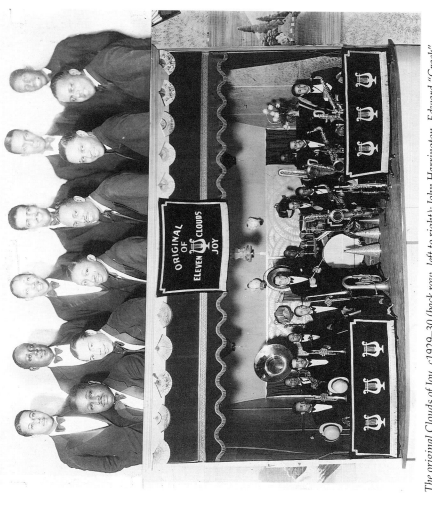

The original Clouds of Joy, c1929–30 (back row, left to right): John Harrington, Edward "Crack" McNeil, Allen Durham, Harry "Big Jim" Lawson, Gene Prince, John Williams; (front row, left to right) Marion Jackson, Billy Massey, Claude Williams, Andy Kirk, Bill Dirvin, Slim Freeman.

Clouds of Joy, California, 1933 (foreground): Andy (clapping), Ben Thigpen (vibes), Mary Lou Williams and Pha Terrell (conducting)

*Kansas City, 1934 (left to right): Mary Lou Williams, John Harrington,
Ben Webster, Pha Terrell, John Williams, Ben Thigpen, Harry "Big Jim" Lawson,
Ted Brinson, Irving "Mouse" Randolph, Andy Kirk, Ted Donnelly,
Earl Thompson.*

*The Clouds of Joy in 1936, at the time of recording "Until the real thing comes
along"*

Pha Terrell, c1935

Mary Lou Williams, 1938

Andy "giving an obscure young trumpeter the chance of a lifetime" (photograph taken at the time Armstrong opened the new Golden Gate Ballroom, New York)

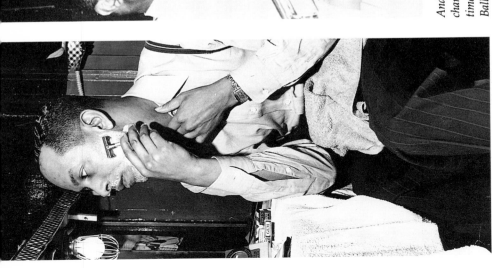

On the road, c1935

"The mad hatters," 1936: various band members, including June Richmond and Mary Lou Williams (seated); Andy is standing second from the right.

The Clouds of Joy, c1940

Floyd "Wonderful" Smith, 1940

Harry "Big Jim" Lawson, 1940s

Dick Wilson, late 1930s

Floyd "Candy" Johnson, who was in the band
1942–7

"June Richmond did a crowd-pleaser in the 1930s. She'd stick just one foot out on the stage, then sneak up on me like a mugger. She'd growl and say, 'I want to dance!' And away we'd go."

June Richmond's version of the cake-walk

Publicity photo of the band during the period it was represented by Joe Glaser

Wartime (left to right): Terry Gibbs, Andy, Chubby Jackson, June Richmond, Tyree Glenn (center front), Ralph Burns, unknown, unknown

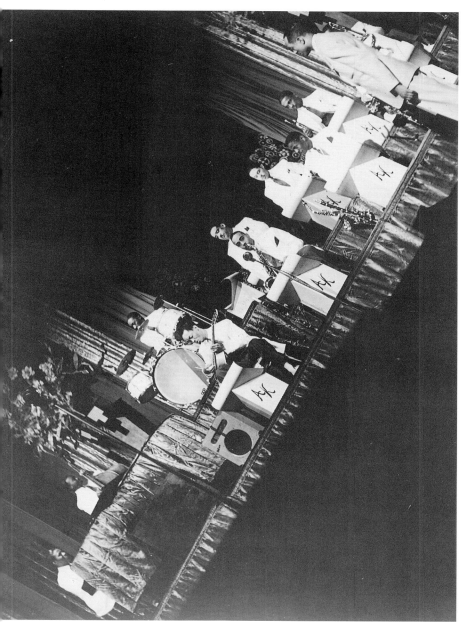

The Clouds of Joy, c1942

The band, mid-1940s

Joe Williams, c1946

Andy, 1940s

...ndy with the impresario Willie Bryant, 1952

Booker Collins, 1940s

The Clouds, 1940s

"I don't remember his name, but this guy was the politest bouncer I ever met –
except maybe for Pha Terrell, who was a bouncer before he was a singer. Pha was
a shrimp, but he could lay out a gorilla."

A shot in a recording studio (left to right): Mary Lou Williams, unknown, Chubby
Jackson, Andy, unknown, June Richmond, unknown

Backstage, 1940s: Andy (center) is flanked by June Richmond and his wife Mary.

A band job at Lake Charles, Louisiana

52nd Street, New York: Curly Howard of the Three Stooges sits in: "I've known stooges who played much worse."

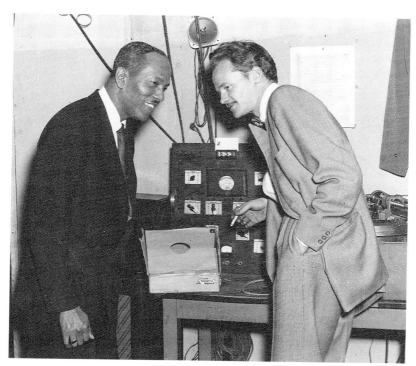

Listening to playbacks

A battle of tenors, Los Angeles, c1945

Andy with Jimmie Crawford and Budd Johnson, 1952

Andy with Jimmy McPartland and (seated) Jimmy Forrest

"Harry Truman, who used to help run Kansas City during its heyday. This is
years later, after he was president. The scene is the Theresa, a fabled Harlem hotel
that I managed for some years. I'm standing second right."

Aging Clouds, 1966

Andy cuts a cake to celebrate the 50th anniversary of the band.

traveling more by bus and I could keep cars longer. I drove that 1940 Buick until 1948, when somebody stole it right by our apartment building here at 555 Edgecombe. Then I bought a Cadillac. That was the end.

You always hear about one-nighters, how awful they were: "Man, those one-nighters are killing me. They're a drag, man." I want to talk about how *good* one-nighters were. If it hadn't been for one-nighters, I wouldn't have met Mrs Mary McLeod Bethune, and Dr George Washington Carver, and a lot of other wonderful people whose names aren't in anybody's "Who's Who." But because of them we could do those one-nighters which were such a necessary part of our business.

We couldn't stay in the white hotels where the white bands stayed. I'm glad now we couldn't. We'd have missed out on a whole country full of folks who put us up in their homes, cooked dinners and breakfasts for us, told us how to get along in Alabama and Mississippi, helped us out in trouble, and became our friends for life. All those "lovely folks we met" – to quote my own lyrics – weren't rich or famous, most of them, but they were heroes and heroines to Andy Kirk and his Twelve Clouds of Joy. And also to all the other colored bands the white folks danced to but kept out of their hotels and restaurants and homes.

Here and there, I have to say, a black door was closed, too. Some homeowners were very particular about who graced – or might have disgraced – their homes. Every time Jo Jones saw me he said, "There were only three musicians Mrs White would take in – Andy Kirk, Jackie Washington, and me." Mrs White lived at 18 Elgin Street, Dayton, Ohio.

If it hadn't been for one-nighters, I wouldn't have known there were any other people but rednecks in the South. I wouldn't have found out that not all white Southerners wanted to put their foot on me. I wouldn't have found out there were Whites in the South I could talk to person to person, man to man. I saw that people in the South were going along with a system. Many were not really prejudiced, but they accepted the southern tradition without really thinking about it. I found a number of white Southerners who only went along with the segregation idea because that was the law. In their hearts they didn't believe in it.

I didn't object so much to segregation in the South. We felt freer with our own people anyway. I was aware of it but had no hang-up about it. "This is their law," I figured, "and I'm not going to be here long." I had a variety of classes in the South to deal with – the richest of the Whites, the middle class, and all classes of Blacks. But no poor Whites or rednecks.

Georgia had its contrasting dance dates. In Atlanta we played four very exclusive white clubs – the Piedmont Driving Club (the one Griffin Bell, former Attorney General in the Carter Administration, belonged to), the Brookhaven and Druid Hill country clubs, and the Jewish Progressive Club. We did all right at all four. The workout we got playing for the very enthusiastic dancers at the Jewish Progressive Club contrasted with our more leisurely pace at Piedmont. On a date at the Piedmont I asked the dance chairman if they wanted to dance between courses at the formal banquet and dance we were playing. He said, "There'll be no music at all during the banquet because you're going to sit here, you and your boys," and he pointed to one of the banquet tables. "And you're going to get some of this good southern cooking. We want you to enjoy it. You don't get that up in New York where you came from." Our table wasn't six feet from his and he kept track of us the whole time, had the waiter bring us everything we needed and wanted.

We also played an exclusive black club, the Top Hat, patronized by bankers and businessmen.

Even then people said about Atlanta, "This city doesn't belong in the South."

In West Point, Georgia, on the other hand, we were the objects of great curiosity. A white organization had brought us in to play for their annual affair. They had also booked us into a local theater for a special afternoon program to defray expenses. When we came to the stage door a half hour or so before show time, we noticed a lot of people lined up across the street. They watched us going in and out, unloading our instruments and music. Apparently puzzled, they'd seem to whisper to each other, then stare at us.

At two o'clock the curtain went up. I raised my baton – and let it fall. We never played a note because nobody came. But the dance at the hotel that night was jammed.

At a ballroom we played in Charleston, South Carolina, people would bring folding chairs and set them up in rows in front of the bandstand for a concert before the dance. They had our records and wanted to hear the same numbers in person. They'd call out their requests, always the newest record first. I remember one man calling out, "Play *Wha-a-a-m, ma-a-an.*" He was saying, "Play *Wham,* man," in his Sea Islands accent. We recorded that in 1940. Once we'd gone through all the requests, the people would fold up their chairs and get ready to dance. This was not part of our contract, but we had to please our public.

The year 1939 marked a certain kind of milestone in my life. We were playing at Lane College in Jackson, Tennessee. A ball-game, as usual, was part of the scene. I was on second base. Four left-handed batters came up and knocked the ball between my legs. That was my last game. At the age of 41 I stopped playing baseball.

Another time we were playing a white ballroom in Walnut Ridge, Arkansas, a dance put on by one of the local organizations. It was almost quitting time. We were going into our closing theme, *Clouds.* A mean-looking character – he'd been drinking – came up to the bandstand, eyed me, and said, "Where do you think you're going?"

"Straight to New Orleans," I said.

"You ain't goin' no place," he snarled. "You're gonna stay here and play and you're gonna like it."

I could have been nasty and said, "Who's gonna make me like it?" But it's when you talk back that trouble starts. I knew it was time to act. I signaled to John Wiliams to keep the music going and I just quietly got off the stand and went to the office in the back. I spoke to the dance committee about this character who was looking for trouble. They went right into action and rounded up five of their members, who then marched up to the bandstand, grabbed the trouble-maker and escorted him out. We went into our theme song again, got paid, and left for New Orleans. No problem.

In Lakeland, Florida, we were playing for a dance at a very exclusive white club, the Lakeland Country Club. When we came in the manager of the club came over to me and said, "My sons have all your records. They're crazy about your band. One plays bass and the other plays drums. Would you do me a big favor? Would you let them sit in and play a number with your band?"

"OK. Sure," I said. "I'd be happy to. They can sit in for a number just before intermission."

When the time came we chose a number they particularly liked. Well, they knew that arrangement note for note. They played their parts perfectly, just the way we recorded it. As they got down from the bandstand I noticed a lot of people congratulating them, patting them on the back, shaking their hands: "I didn't know you could play like that!"

"Boy, you're real pros!"

Their father was beaming, so pleased with how they'd performed.

Six months later we were playing a black dance at City Auditorium in Atlanta. Whites were up in the balcony listening. Whites always came and sat in the balcony at black dances, and vice versa. During intermission a white man came down from the balcony, walked over to me, and said, "Remember me?"

"I know your face," I said.

"I was the manager of Lakeland Country Club."

I noticed the past tense. "Was?"

"Yes," he said. "Was. I got fired because I let my sons get on the bandstand and play with you and your band. They reminded me this act was not in harmony with southern tradition."

Southern tradition had many different nuances. We were playing for a dance at The Pines, an exclusive white club in

Opelousas, Louisiana – Lousyana, as one of the boys in the band said. At intermission the owner came out on the bandstand and spoke into the mike. "Andy's been here a number of times, as you know," he said. "Let him know how much we love him down here." Strong applause. "See, Andy, we all love you," he said, "and any time you come through here, I want you to call me and say hello."

It so happened we came through again in another few months, and I called him.

"Where are you?" he asked.

"I'm down at the colored restaurant."

"I know," he said. "I'll be right down and get you." He arrived in about ten minutes, and while the boys were eating he drove me to his home in a nice white section of town. The house was on a corner, so the front door was on one street and the kitchen door on the other.

He parked at the side of the house and we went in the kitchen door, and then through the house into the living room. Now usually a living room is open only to your family and close friends. His wife greeted me, and they both invited me to sit down. We chatted a while. He asked me how the music was going, bragged again how much they always enjoyed it when we played at The Pines. After 15 or 20 minutes I said, "The boys'll be through eating and we'll have to be getting on our way."

As we got up he said, "You're always welcome in Opelousas. And whenever we have a dance and you're available, we want you, because we love you and your band." We left the living room, went back to the kitchen, out the kitchen door, and he drove me back to the restaurant. His heart was in the right place. He just didn't want his neighbors to see me coming through the front door. Overall thinking in the South, I discovered, was that Whites didn't want their neighbors to think they were liberal.

Bandleaders are not as a rule businessmen. I depended on Joe Glaser for our routes and jobs: "You go to so-and-so, I'm getting you so much money." He was the one who dealt with the bus companies when we traveled by bus. People may wonder if we were exploited by agents. We all were. In contracts. The bookers and managers had their own lawyers who were ours, too. That didn't make sense. Glaser got his cut, the territory booker got his cut, the ballroom or location got their cut. We had what was left. But we were happy to be playing, so we didn't think too much about the money.

We couldn't play white hotels then. The hotel jobs were good because they had radio wires, and usually a band stayed in a hotel spot for a long time – years sometimes. But those spots were controlled by white agents and so white bands got them. Another thing, those bands usually played the hotel-society style. I didn't particularly like that, but I did think it was nice to be able to stay in a spot year after year like some white bands did.

There was one black band who did have a long-term hotel spot – and in Texas, too: Alphonso Trent at the Adolphus in Dallas. The only other one I knew of was George Morrison and his long stay at the Albany Hotel in Denver.

But, as I said before, one-nighters were a necessary part of our business, and there was lots that was good about them. The band promoters and bookers usually told you where you could stay. For us it was "across the tracks." The tracks were always the dividing line. There was a regular network of homes and small black hotels across the country, north and south. Like Ann Johnson in Boston. She had rooms to rent over her restaurant called Mom's Lunch.

"Where you stayin'?"

"Mom's Lunch."

"Not the Waldorf. Homier."

A man named Clark, a railway mail clerk, put us up in Jacksonville, Florida. He ran the post office at the railroad station and was a jazz and record buff. I remember a woman in Shreveport whose house was as clean and shining as the washing and ironing she did for a living. I was there the night of a Joe Louis fight. I asked her if she wouldn't like to listen to it on the radio with me. She said she would, but she stayed out in the kitchen for the first few rounds. As it got closer, the announcer was excitedly describing the action:

"It's a left, a right, another left . . . " She came in just then. "I thought you'd decided not to hear the fight after all," I said.

"Oh, no," she said. "I just don't bother till it gets to that 'left, right, left, right'."

We stayed with a hard-working family in Monroe, Louisiana, named Willis. They owned a dairy. Milking time seemed to be all the time.

Some of the little hotels were nice; some were not so nice or so clean. One we stayed in in New Orleans was not much of a hotel, but it gave me a front-row seat on a local custom I'd heard about but had never seen. Sunday morning I woke up to the music of a brass band. I got up, looked out and saw a funeral passing by. The band was dressed in uniforms and marching very slowly. The music was like a dirge. Women dressed in white skirts walked solemnly in front of the band. Quite a crowd followed along the street. Some time later they all came back, dancing and shouting, and the band was blowing *When the saints go marching in,* up-tempo and all-out. And now those women in the white skirts were really strutting.

If it hadn't been for one-nighters, I might never have seen a New Orleans funeral parade.

Even after things eased up we still stayed in those places, because we had made friends there. We got close to people that way. It was the same when Mary and Bernice and I went to Europe in 1961. We stayed in the pensions so we could be close to the people.

One night when we arrived in Dallas on a trip west from Jacksonville, Florida, I had a terrific toothache. A friend had introduced me to a young dentist in Jacksonville, but his treatment hadn't solved the problem, and by the time we hit Dallas the tooth was killing me. A friend of Mary's and mine from Denver had married a Dr Burke, a dentist, and they had settled in Dallas. I called them after the job and, in spite of the fact that it was then 2:00 a.m., Dr Burke took me to his office and pulled out that tooth. There were quite a few black professional people in Dallas, not as many as in Kansas City, but enough for me to notice, because they always came to the dances we played for in the Dallas–Fort Worth area.

We made friends with many of our loyal fans, and many, like Dr Burke, were there to help in times of trouble. That's why I say it was more than a business.

Even famous Blacks like Dr George Washington Carver acted as Good Samaritans. If I hadn't been ill in Opelika, Alabama, I wouldn't have met Dr Carver. I had gone to a doctor in the town but he didn't seem to know what the trouble was. He advised me to go into Tuskegee and see Dr Carver, who at that time was at Tuskegee Institute. I did, and when I met him he came up to me, looked into my face for a moment and – even though he wasn't a medical doctor, but a botanist – knew just what to do.

And, speaking of Alabama, whenever we played black dances in Birmingham it was the custom for a policeman to be on hand. Of course the police then were all white. Our white policeman, Mr Styles, was very nice. We even exchanged Christmas cards. As long as we were over on the black side and stayed there, we saw only the good side of Mr Styles.

We were passing through Birmingham one time and drove by the Tutweiler Hotel, the Waldorf Astoria of Birmingham. And there was our Mr Styles out in front directing traffic. "Hey, stop," I called to our bus driver. "There's my friend." He pulled over, and I got out and walked into the middle of the street to talk to Mr Styles. "Hey, Mr Styles, hello," I called.

He said nothing, kept his back to me and went on directing traffic. He didn't want to be seen talking with me, or even saying hello. The boys saw the whole thing from the bus and fell out laughing. That's the way it was then. Three years or so ago the black Elks took over the Tutweiler for their convention. "What a difference a day makes."

A couple of other Birmingham experiences come to mind. There was a gas station there where we bought gas once in a while. After we'd played a dance one night we stopped there, and Ben Thigpen, our drummer, went in to ask if he could use the rest room. He knew the right approach. He

just asked the man politely, "May I use your rest room?"
Standard procedure was buy gas, go to the rest room.

The man said, "Where you from, boy?"

Ben said, "Laurel, Mississippi."

The man answered, "I knowed it. I could tell. Yes, you go ahead. You can use it. Any time you're down here. But them other smart alecks, I ain't never goin' let them use it."

We were playing the Pickwick Club in the five-point area of Birmingham. There was a Real Southern Gentleman there. Nearly all white Real Southern Gentleman are a certain recognizable type, and they look you over carefully when they know you're from the North. This Real Southern Gentleman at the Pickwick came up to me between sets and said, "Say, Andy, any boys in your band from the Deep South?"

"I was born in Kentucky," I said.

"No," he said, "I mean the *Deep* South."

"We've got a trumpet player from Round Rock, Texas, and our drummer back there, Ben Thigpen, he's from Laurel, Mississippi."

"Good Lord," he said. "Look here, y'all, Andy's got a niggah from Mississippi in his band." He went back and sat down at the table with his party. They apparently got into a discussion about bands. Don Redman and various other bands had been there recently. The table was near enough the bandstand so that I could see the Real Southern Gentleman arguing with one of the women, though I couldn't hear what they were saying.

After the next set he came over again and said, "She," indicating the one he'd been arguing with, "she said Don Redman had a better trombone player than you have. You know what I said to her? I said, 'You're a lah-hr (liar). And you know why? 'Cause Andy's got a niggah from Mississippi in his band.'"

That argument didn't have anything to do with Redman's music and mine. I was better because I had someone from the Deep South in the band. If someone calls me nigger, I'd rather hear a Southerner say it than anyone north of the

Mason–Dixon line. It has a different meaning in the South. "Nigger" is their terminology. And that reminds me of the time we were playing a black dance at a ballroom in Baton Rouge. It was packed and a lot of people were standing around the bandstand. Suddenly I felt a prick in my leg and saw blood there. A tussle started near the stand. I heard someone say, "A man stuck him with a knife."

Then I saw the man with the knife, walking away and growling, "That ole nigger thinks he's cute."

I put on a Band Aid and we went right into the next set.

During a white dance we played in Newport News, Virginia, a couple came up to the bandstand, and the girl started talking to me. The girls were always the fresh ones, they did most of the talking. "I love your band," she said. "I have lots of your records." She named one of her favorites.

"Well, thank you," I said, "but that's Jimmie Lunceford's record."

"It is not," she said indignantly, "it's yours."

The guy with her said, "I guess the man knows what record is his and what isn't."

She was furious then and said to him, "Are you going to take *his* word against mine?"

His face turned red. He took her arm and said, "Come on," and they walked away.

Would he take my word against hers – even though I did know my own records!

Those were the incidents we had to watch out for and retreat from. Our experience had prepared us, especially those years we had made our living in white ballrooms in Oklahoma. There was always someone there to keep you in line so that customers, mostly the girls, didn't create opportunities for you to get out of your place. As long as we were there as servants, we were treated well. On every job the message got to us in one way or another: "Keep your place. You're here as servants. Please the customers, and everything will be fine."

One time Billy Sharpe, our road manager, and I were driving in Columbus, Mississippi, about 2:00 a.m., just after finishing a job there. I was going very carefully, about eight miles an hour. A cop spotted me, came alongside and turned his flashlight into the car on me. "What's your hurry?" he said.

"Oh, I'm in no hurry," I said. "That's why I was going so slowly."

"Where you going?"

"I'm driving Mr Sharpe here to his hotel." Billy was white.

"Well, come along with me." We followed the cop to the courthouse. It was one of those courthouses with a long flight of steps in front. The cop had a big long key he used to unlock the front door. We went in. He talked with the cop on duty, then brought out a bottle of whiskey. "Like a drink?" he asked me.

"No thanks," I said. "I don't drink."

He asked Sharpe and Sharpe also said, "No thanks." He poured himself and the other cop drinks, then said to me, "That'll be $11." So we had to pay $11 for their drinks. Otherwise we'd have had to appear in court next morning. By paying our "fine" we could go, and they wouldn't know where or anything else about us, though I knew he knew we'd been playing a dance there the night before.

I knew a Mr Wright, a white man, who owned a club in Miami and had a black man, Tom Bell, running it for him. After Wright died the club went to his son Stewart, who knew nothing about the business and had to learn it from Tom Bell. As a result they became close business associates. They were in the car together one day, Tom was driving, and pulled up at a traffic light just as the caution flashed. There were two white lines marking off the walk space for pedestrians. Their front wheels were just over the first white line. A cop saw it and came over to the car. "Do you know what those white lines mean?" he asked.

Tom said, "Yes, it's for pedestrians."

The cop spoke to Stewart. "Is this your chauffeur?"

Stewart said, "No, he's a friend. We're friends."

The cop took them in and fined them $100 for fraternizing. That was the law then. I think a lot of white Southerners didn't like the law, but they obeyed it.

There were only three places I felt free to go in and shop in the South: the stores on Lincoln Road, Miami Beach; Muse's in Atlanta, my favorite store; and the White House Department Store in San Antonio. You could shop in those stores and be treated just like anyone else, and you could ride on their elevators. I avoided stores in Birmingham and other places. I heard we had to ride in the freight elevators and I wouldn't take a chance.

There was one time in Durham, North Carolina, when a white man made a remark I considered insulting and I left the room. Six months later we were back there playing a dance. He was there and came up to me, shook my hand, said he was glad to see me, and made no reference to the incident. He asked me if I was staying overnight and when I said, yes, he said, "Look, why don't you come and stay at my house. I've got plenty of room. Be glad to have you." In all the stories I'd heard about the South, I'd never heard of a black man staying overnight as a guest in a white man's house. He broke the tradition he was brought up with to invite me to be his house guest. And I accepted. I wanted to show him I appreciated him as a man, that I didn't hold the insulting remark he once made against him. He had already left for his office when I came down the next morning. And when his black cook saw me she nearly turned white from the shock.

7

Those wheels were still rolling

Next session in the study those wheels were still rolling, carrying Andy Kirk and the Twelve Clouds of Joy "north, east, south, and west," and college campuses were as familiar to them as ballrooms and lodgings "across the tracks."

We played colleges from Yale and Harvard in New England to Syracuse and Cornell in upstate New York, to Wisconsin, Purdue and Kansas Aggies in the Middle West and Atlanta, Emory, Bethune Cookman and Tuskegee in the South. At one fall get-together at Penn State there were 52 bands at the different sorority and fraternity houses. And the kids went from house to house, dancing to all those different bands. Talk about battles of music! That 52-band bash must have eclipsed any contest ever. I thought it was something when we were one of five bands at the Golden Gate Ballroom in New York, with a 16-voice choir besides. It was a tribute to W. C. Handy and a high point of the evening came when we all played our versions of *St Louis Blues* in succession. But nothing could compare with that Penn State weekend of music.

One year we had a rather spectacular series of dates at Emory University in Atlanta. We played the hops and proms of each class – freshman, sophomore, junior and senior – all the same year.

At Texas A & M and Arkansas State we stayed in the fraternity houses. The dance committee at Texas A & M had one specific guideline for me: "Play anything you want to play except *Deep in the Heart of Texas*."

On our way to Arkansas State at Fayetteville one time we stopped at a white restaurant along the road. The whole band was hungry and we decided to risk it. I went in to ask if it was OK, and told the lady in charge how many of us there were. She said, "Sure, come right in."

We sat down at a big table and were served a full course dinner. As soon as we'd finished up the vegetables or potatoes or whatever, she'd bring on fresh helpings. It was the kind of service we called "pitch till you win." In other words, "eat till you're filled." That taught me a lesson: all Whites are not the same, anymore than all Blacks are the same.

We often played for black dances at the armory in Durham, North Carolina. The balcony was always full of white college kids from Duke University and the University of North Carolina at Chapel Hill. They had our records and liked to come and hear us in person. On one of our dates the place was full of college kids, more than ever it seemed. Pha Terrell was singing ballads. He was only 5'9" and weighed only 160 pounds soaking wet. There was a big black man at the front of the bandstand scowling at Pha. You could see he didn't like his looks or the way he sang in falsetto – sounded to him like a fag, I guess. All of sudden, he grabbed the standing mike and shoved it into Pha's face. But Pha caught it and went right on singing. He finished his chorus and stepped back to let the band play half a chorus. I moved the mike back, but when Pha turned towards the crowd to sing the last half he took the mike and put it right down in the black man's face to challenge him, so he could reach it and shove it at Pha again. But Pha had a good grip on it, and as he took his bows he must have called the man a dirty name, because that big fellow jumped on the stand. But before he could draw back to hit Pha, "little" 5'9" Pha laid him out with one punch. The kids in the balcony were cheering. They could see the knockout punch and wanted more. Everybody else was applauding.

Pha may have looked small and defenseless, and a lot of men didn't like him because women swooned over him, but he could have taken on just about anybody. You remember he had been a bouncer at the little club in Kansas City where I first saw him and heard him sing *Lullaby of the Leaves*.

We had another little scrape involving Pha, in Brownsville,

Pennsylvania, just south of Pittsburgh, where we were playing a black dance – mostly miners. The girl-friend of one of the miners had come to the dance by herself. She hung around the stand, wanted to meet Pha. I introduced her to him, and he invited her to have a drink. They went to the bar on the balcony and stood there in plain sight. Apparently her boy-friend had spies around. Ben Thigpen started his long drum roll – that's how we always got the signal to come back on the stand. He hit a cymbal and went into a rhythm beat. Dick Wilson grabbed his tenor and started playing, one by one the boys got on the stand, and Pha and the girl started across the floor towards us. Out of nowhere her boy-friend came charging towards them. Pha walked close to him, holding him by the arm, trying to explain he had merely invited the girl to have a drink out of courtesy after she had approached him. But the boy-friend got angrier and louder, so Pha hauled off and socked him. And down he went.

I went to the police station down the block and explained what had happened. A squad car with three or four cops followed me back to see that no trouble started. They let me know they'd take Pha to the station to avoid any more scenes. People thought he'd been arrested. It cooled things off. We picked him up after the job and left. All quiet on the coal front.

We played another coal mining town – Lynch, Kentucky, on the border of West Virginia in the Appalachians – where I saw scrip for the first time. The men in the family I stayed with worked in the mines and everyone used this scrip at the company store. The band got paid in cash – real money.

During our early years in and around New York we played a date at the Pearl Theater in Philadelphia, where Blanche Calloway was also appearing – but not with her own band. I told you about playing stand-in for Fletcher Henderson's band at that debutante party in Cincinnati. Well, now we were disguised by the theater manager as Blanche Calloway's Joy Boys for a recording date with Blanche. All the while his henchmen were manipulating this arrangement, the manager was inviting me to relax in his office. He'd say,

"Here, sit in this nice, soft chair. Be comfortable. You shouldn't have to stay down in the basement with the rest of the band."

But I knew what was happening. The boys in the band reported everything that was going on.

We played the Savoy Ballroom many times. Social and fraternal clubs could rent it on Wednesday nights. Thursday was maid's night out and that's when the boys and girls flocked to "the Home of Happy Feet."

Jewish employment agencies in New York recruited girls in the South and brought them north to work as domestics in New York and the surrounding suburbs. Years later many of those same girls, married and with families, would come up to me at dances and talk about hearing us at the Savoy. Invariably the husbands would say, "I met my wife at the Savoy. When you played *Until the real thing comes along*, that did it."

When we came into the Apollo Theater on 125th Street in Harlem for the first time we got another of those cool New York greetings. Tom Whalen, the music director, always rehearsed the shows first, then the bands. In those days bands were in the pit. The day of our opening he rehearsed the show, then disappeared. We had to get through the performance as best we could. But the people didn't care. They came to hear *Real Thing*. We got a tremendous reception. We were something different, a western band. The prevailing style there was Fletcher Henderson's – fast tunes, jump things. We came in with a smoother style and a four-beat. Andy Kirk was the new kid in town.

On another occasion I was a somewhat unpopular figure with the Apollo management. The RKO Palace in midtown was planning to have a vaudeville house in Harlem – the Alhambra at Seventh Avenue and 126th Street. It would play the same show featured downtown. An RKO official wanted a name band and the only one he knew was Noble Sissle. Off the top of his head the president of Local 802 told him, "You can't get a better band than Andy Kirk."

When the deal was set the Apollo owner said to me,

"You'll never work in my theater again." It looked like competition around the corner.

I said, "Well, thank you."

I was at the Alhambra a couple of months. Part of the job was to go down to the Palace and check out the show. I enjoyed it.

As winter melted slowly into early spring once more and the first hints of leaves began to appear on the trees across from 555 Edgecombe, so changes were taking place in the itineraries and locations of the Clouds of Joy under the darkening clouds of World War II.

We were playing at the Tune Town Ballroom in St Louis when the Japanese bombed Pearl Harbor on 7 December 1941. It was a Sunday matinee dance and loaded with GIs from the camp near there. They had been in training and were preparing to go home soon. I talked to a lot of them. They'd tell me, "I saw you at such-and-such a place. I have all your records." Things like that. "I'll be goin' home." They thought the call-up was for a year only. Instead, I had to announce that they had orders to report back to camp immediately.

As the war progressed we were doing more and more camps. On our way from California to play a camp in Yuma, Arizona, we had to cross the Colorado River at Yuma. There was a toll-bridge, and if you were on government detail the toll-booth man always passed you through without charging the toll. This guy in the toll-booth saw we were a black band and made us pay. We explained our mission but his answer was, "If you don't like this country, why don't you move out?"

On a trip from San Francisco to Wells, Nevada, we took the Southern Pacific, and at Wells we had to take a bus to Twin Falls, Idaho. We had quite a wait for that bus. Wells was a small town. There was a bar but no restaurant near the depot, so the fellows said, "Might as well get a drink." They went into the bar and got this from the bartender, "I can't serve you."

"Why not?"

"It's against the boss's rules."

Then one of the boys began his "sermon": "Don't you know there's a war on? Those bullets aren't gonna pick out who's black and who's white. We're serving our country, why can't you serve us?"

"You know, you're right," he said. "That's my boss's rule, but I'll serve you."

There was no cursing or getting mad. They just reasoned with him. Back in school in Denver I learned I could deal with situations through reasoning. I found Whites who would listen.

We had played in Little Rock, Arkansas, and were going to Jackson, Mississippi, on the Illinois Central. Because of the war, manpower was short and there was no steward on the diner. In his place was a black man as "waiter in charge," Mr Smith. But he was doing the steward's job, whatever his title or pay.

There were 20 of us and we traveled together because we were playing the camps and had to keep rank, so to speak. Billy Sharpe had gone to the station-master and explained, "We have a big group, and we've got to get on because we have to play a camp at Jackson." We got an official OK. When we boarded the train at Little Rock it was loaded, but we went as usual to the Jim Crow car up front.

Mr Smith started there to give first call for dinner. When he saw our big group, he said, "Come on back and we'll feed you first." In those days there were curtains in diners to use when the southbound trains crossed the Mason–Dixon line. They were always pulled across the dining car to separate the Blacks from the Whites. We took up 20 seats so the diner was pretty full already. After first call was made Whites were lining up at the doorway waiting to be served.

The conductor came through and pulled the curtain across to hide us. The waiter in charge pulled it open. The conductor yanked it across again and said, "I want you to know" – and he was shaking his finger at Mr Smith – "I'm in charge of this train from the engine to the last car."

The waiter in charge said, "And I want you to know,"

pointing his finger right back at the conductor, "I'm in charge of this car from the kitchen to the other end! And if you don't want this car on your train, put it on the side track." And he opened the curtain with a yank. The dining car stayed on, the curtain stayed open, the train rolled on.

It may have looked like a protest, but Mr Smith's main concern was to give service. He was in charge and determined to give the best service possible. With his reduced staff he couldn't take care of all the diners and have his waiters constantly pulling that curtain back and forth. But this kind of confrontation would never have happened before the war. It showed the changing attitude on the part of Blacks. In fact, you could see a different attitude developing in both Blacks and Whites. They were beginning to ask questions about the whole Jim Crow situation.

We had incident after incident to point that up. For instance, we were playing a white dance in a big warehouse in Montgomery, Alabama, and who should come in but Joe Bushkin. He was stationed there with the air force, along with some other New York musicians we knew. At intermission we were really fraternizing – shaking hands, hugging each other, like old buddies. Finally, this cracker who'd been watching got closer and closer so he could hear what we were saying. You could tell by the look on his face he couldn't understand how Bushkin and I could be so friendly on a social basis. One of the other musicians with him made a crack about being in "good old Dixie." The cracker heard that and picked me out to talk to. "Tell me," he said, "why is it these fellows, when they're down here, they always have something smart to say about us?"

Bushkin answered for me, "Because you won't give up."

Some of the same musicians came down to the bus station to see us off the next morning. We were all on the bus-station side and about eight or ten natives were on the opposite side. First there had been just two, then two more stopped to see what was going on, until finally that little crowd had gathered. And there they stood and watched until we got on the bus. You could just tell what they were thinking: "What white boys doing there? What have they got so much in common with those niggers?"

Jazz was an influence on all musicians. It gave us something in common. There was more fraternizing because of the music.

We were doing the Coca Cola show in Portsmouth, Virginia. We did a lot of them across the country. It was a sailor's place. We did a segregated show because it was the thought of the officer-in-charge to have two shows, one for Blacks and one for Whites, so they wouldn't sit together. The black cook there said to me, "Don't feel bad, Andy, but none of us will be there. The officer thinks this is a social gathering. He forgets we are at war."

At our first show the black sailors in the audience were mostly from Chicago. They let the officer-in-charge know what they thought of his policies by cutting up the tires on his car. He spoke to me later. "They shouldn't have done that. They know where they are."

Some did time for it. But I saw their side. They had to protest.

The war brought new attitudes towards nearly everything. My original band rules – and they were not strict, but important – didn't work. My three basic rules were: no fighting, no drinking on the stand, be on time. I realized some couldn't drink and play, though some could. If we weren't on time it would be breaking our contract. Say the contract called for 14, then all 14 must be on the stand and ready to play at nine, or whatever time we started. If one man was late the contract was in jeopardy.

Jimmie Lunceford was like a sergeant. He checked the socks. In my band, if anyone forgot the white handkerchief in the breast pocket there was no wrist-slapping. Lunceford had been a professor, he was strict. The guys in the band he started with and made a hit with around Buffalo, New York, were all the high-school kids he'd taught in Memphis. And he and Henry Wells and Ed Wilcox were all in college together at Fisk.

But, as I say, my original rules didn't work. We were

changing men fast and they all came in with their own thinking. They'd be drinking and clowning and were not accustomed to the decorum and standards I thought were right. The style of music was changing. Bop was coming in and taking over. Boppers were the only musicians we could get who weren't going to war. Howard McGhee was the first of that group to come on the band. He had his own style, but he could play other things. This was the time all the younger musicians were beginning to express themselves.

One night I got disgusted with all the carrying-on and at intermission I said, "I want everyone in the band room after we're through." They all came in like school boys. "What's the matter with you fellows?" I asked them.

J. D. King raised his hand, like school kids do. "You know something's wrong with us," he said. "We're all 4Fs."

I had to change some of my attitude. But my original requirements were not stringent. I didn't want regimentation. The band did wear uniforms, but I didn't worry about the color of the socks. It wasn't the army. I like harmony. We had to feel harmony with one another. It was the feel of the band that mattered. We went out socially together. We had our softball team. I couldn't be a Napoleon. I had too much feeling for people.

We were to take the C&0 from Hampton, Virginia, to Roanoke. Billy Sharpe arranged for us to get on the first section because that section had a diner. We couldn't use a bus on account of gas rationing. There were so many of us the conductor was mad. "You should have been on the other section," he barked. We couldn't do anything about it, but he certainly showed his anger. When we got off at Roanoke J. D. King said, "I have one thing to say to you. If I had you up North, I'd mop up this ground with you."

After J. D. left the band he settled in Los Angeles. I saw him there a few years ago when Mary and I went to my niece's wedding. We went into a bear hug. He remembered breaking up my meeting with the band with his "We're all 4Fs." And he confessed, "I couldn't hold a horn with those other guys," meaning Jimmy Forrest and Ed Loving. "And I couldn't make it on showmanship."

I certainly didn't agree that he couldn't hold a horn with Forrest and Loving. I called them "the Three Horsemen." They did a number where they "battled," and the audience was like an audience at a prize-fight. While Forrest and Loving were fighting it out, chorus after chorus, J. D would engage in some stage business, say to me, "Why do you let them play so long?" Then he'd take up his music and start to go off, with me after him. I'd get him back for his turn. He didn't play long – but what he played! He broke up every audience, particularly those at the Plantation Club in Los Angeles, where we played in 1945.

We met up with June Richmond there. She was appearing in an act. She had been our dynamite vocalist around 1939 into 1943. I had gotten her out of the Jimmy Dorsey band. We played a dance with Jimmy at Manhattan Center in New York after June had joined me. She was a Muhammad Ali – "I'm the greatest. Hand me that mike!" She had so much self-confidence. That night she did *Darktown Strutters' Ball* and had the house rocking. Poor Helen O'Connell wouldn't come on after that and Bob Eberly had to sing alone for a while.

Joe Glaser advanced money to June to buy a house in Hollywood. She had two daughters and she pretended she wanted to make a home for them. She really wanted to go out on her own.

Even though *Real Thing* was synonymous with our band and was the means of our breakthrough from race records, as far as I recall some of the sides June Richmond did with us, like *Hey Lawdy, Mama,* were even bigger sellers.

June was also the cause of Mary Lou Williams leaving the band in 1942. We were playing a date in Washington DC, and at some point during the evening Mary Lou got up from the piano and walked out. I didn't even know she'd left. We sometimes had to play without the piano, as when one was so out of tune she would give up on it rather than try to transpose all night. As the war spread, so did out-of-tune pianos. Only the best ballrooms now kept them in good tune. When out, they were usually too low to tune our horns to A, so we'd have to tune them to B instead. That meant Mary Lou had to transpose every number. I can hear her now, playing a chord or two on each piano as we came on a job, and saying, "I guess I'll have to transpose all night."

That night in Washington, she not only got up and left the piano and whatever disagreements or clashes there'd been with June, she also kept on going all the way home to Pittsburgh.

We had a succession of worthy successors – Hank Jones, Johnny Young, Ken Kersey. We did *Boogie Woogie Cocktail* with Ken at the Apollo – I did play there again! – and tore the house down. He, of course, played heavier than Mary Lou. No woman can play as heavy as a man – at least none that I know of.

Other great jazzmen were in and out of the band during the war, men like Eddie "Lockjaw" Davis on tenor and Fats Navarro on trumpet. I always think of a club we played in St Louis in connection with Fats Navarro. A man came in one night from across the river in East St Louis, Illinois, with a roll of brand new 20-dollar bills. He had a request: *Beer Barrel Polka*. Fats said out loud to me, "Man, we don't want to play all that old corny stuff." Before this, no one in the band ever spoke out like that. I ignored it and we played *Beer Barrel Polka*. And we played it again. And again. Each time we'd get a 20-dollar bill. I would never hide tips, just put the money out on John Harrington's music stand.

We played *Beer Barrel Polka* 12 times. I was sick of it, too, and felt it was unfair to the other guests. So I called intermission. Fats said, "Man, we don't need no intermission." How $240 had changed his mind!

Fats was a brilliant musician but plenty mixed up. I knew his father, and I tried to talk to Fats, get him to see how he was getting himself loused up. He didn't know any better. He got in with the wrong characters. He died at age 26 or 27. Seeing him laid out in the chapel, those characters said, "That's a drag, man," and then would go out and shoot up.

The tone of Andy's voice indicated his incomprehension of such behavior – musicians going right on indulging a habit that had done in one of their fellow musicians. That incomprehension extended also to another kind of musician-to-musician behavior he found hard to excuse.

With a couple of exceptions I've never really disliked anyone. But there was one white leader who asked me to come to his apartment one day. I had only recently met him and couldn't figure out why he wanted to see me. Reluctantly I went. He had lost his guitarist, so he proposed that my great guitarist, Floyd Smith, leave me and go with him, and so how about releasing him. "He's a man in his own right," I said. "Why do you ask me? He's not my slave. Why don't you ask him?"

Floyd Smith did not go with that leader.

At a white dance we played in Clearwater, Florida, there was a fellow who kept walking back and forth in front of the bandstand looking at me. It was not a happy look. I knew he wanted to talk to me. I could always tell by people's movements whether they wanted to say something to me. "Have you a request?" I finally asked him.

"Yeah," he said. "I want to talk to you at intermission."

His friends kept trying to pull him away, making signs to me that he was drunk. When I met him at intermission he said he had a letter from his brother who was in the Marines and had been on Okinawa. Black Marines had saved the day there. He showed me the letter. It said, "Don't let anybody tell you anything about those niggers. One of them saved my life." After I'd read it he put it back in the envelope and said, "And my brother's no lah-hr (liar)."

Atlanta always held encouraging signs of progress. At one dance we played there, a banker came up to me at intermission and asked if I knew a certain colored man that worked at his bank. "Sure," I said. "I just saw him today at Ma Sutton's." Ma Sutton had a restaurant and rooms to rent right in the heart of blacktown, in the 300-block of Auburn Avenue, right off the main business section of the city. That's where I stayed and had my meals. Her biggest business came from Whites, but it was one place Blacks and

Whites mingled. It had an up-and-coming atmosphere about it. I remember the waitresses wore white aprons and caps.

After the war we ran into more changes that affected our bookings in some places. As a result of some civil rights law that I was unaware of, we were being refused jobs we'd played over and over in Pennsylvania, like Lakewood, Lakeside, Mahoney City, Wilkes Barre, Carbondale, Berwick, Sunbury, and Pottsville. Ballroom owners didn't say it, but they were afraid that if they used us they'd get the colored coal miners as customers, and they didn't want that business.

We were coming back from one Pennsylvania tour to New York, traveling on Route 30, and stopped at a restaurant where the buses all stopped. When I looked at the menu the waiter gave me, I said, "Isn't this a mistake? We ate on our last stop in Pittsburgh and there were no prices like this. This must be the wrong menu."

The waiter shook his head. "Boss's orders." He looked at his watch. "It's two o'clock in the morning, so what's the difference? Who's gonna know? I'll charge you the same as everyone else. Here's the regular menu." They had made up a special one for colored folks. They were afraid Blacks would be running into their restaurant and they'd have to enforce that civil rights law.

We had played the Arcadia Ballroom in New York many times. Joe Glaser told the manager, Hugh Corrigan, that we would be coming into town and Hugh said, "Fine, Andy always does a good job." For some reason Joe wanted me to go see Corrigan, so I dropped in at the ballroom at 53rd and Broadway one day and told the ticket man I would like to see Mr Corrigan.

Two bouncers in tuxes came towards me. Mr Corrigan was on the balcony and signaled to the ticket man that it was all right and motioned me up. It was hard for me to believe my ears when he said, "Andy, my owners feel that because of the new civil rights law, you'll now be drawing people from Harlem. It's not me, you understand, but my owners don't want that business, so I have to cancel the contract."

Though we were running into new problems like this, we were still making tours around the country and at the same time amassing information about places where Blacks could stay for Travelguide, a New York company. Mary was treasurer of it during the war. I told Travelguide about all the little black hotels and homes where we stayed, and that way Blacks traveling in different parts of the country had a reference book to guide them out of embarrassing situations. Billy Butler, the head of Travelguide, could confidently proclaim, "Vacation, recreation, without humiliation."

In 1948 the band was in a movie called *Killer Diller*. It was a comedy, and made at Pathé studios on East 116th Street. Convenient for me, because Mary and I had moved into 555 Edgecombe several years before – 1939 – so New York had been home-base since then. I didn't see the movie. I wasn't excited about it. I never got excited about big names and all that.

But Andy finally did see that movie. In a phone conversation I had with him on 30 March 1980 he said he and Mary and Bernice had seen it "a couple of months ago" at the Thalia on Broadway and 95th Street, and that Butterfly McQueen was in it. They had paid regular admission to get in, but word got around that he was there, and at the end of the movie he and Miss McQueen – who apparently was there also – were called up on stage for a question-and-answer session. "We also got our admission fee refunded," he said.

John Williams and I, with an eye to a little extra income, had opened the Kansas City Barbecue at 129th Street and Seventh Avenue. We imported a chef from Kansas City to give it authenticity. Our best customers were Red Norvo and Mildred Bailey. John was out of the band by then, but I was still on the road, so Mary and John ran the barbecue. Mary was on daytimes, John evenings. He was my "straw boss," but John was something of a gambler and we were having trouble keeping our records straight, so I gave the business to him, and he closed it up.

I also took time out to buy a little house for my aunt in Denver, on Lafayette Street, near 2410 Marion that was the first house she had owned. Luther Walton, my old Sunday

School teacher, was a building contractor, and I engaged him to build on an extra room and put in hardwood floors. I paid cash for that house. It had been part of an estate that dated back to 1850. There was a history that came with it, telling who had owned it and many details about its past life. The house was brick inside and paneled with wood over the brick. I had new paneling put in, a gas stove, an automatic floor furnace, and a new roof. There was a 20-foot living room, a small kitchen, and one bedroom always made up and ready for Andrew. Flowers bloomed in the little garden at the side of the house from May to November. The house was at least one small way I could let my aunt know how thankful I was for her home training that enabled me to have little jobs during school, and later to realize a wonderful career in music.

By 1949 the spokes by which we had first traveled out of Kansas City had reached to the farthest corners of the country – over 300 cities in nearly every state (never did get to Vermont) and into Ontario, Manitoba and British Columbia, Canada. Our farthest north date in Maine was Orchard Beach, and the farthest north of all, Ironton, Michigan, on Lake Superior. Our farthest south spot was Key West, Florida, in the East, and San Diego, California, in the West. El Paso, Texas, was our farthest west date, and farthest northwest was Vancouver, British Columbia.

We were in Rocky Mount, North Carolina, to play the June German in 1949. The June German was a festival celebration like the Fourth of July. Former Tar Heels, black and white, came from as far away as Boston and Chicago to renew old times and ties. The town was so crowded there were not enough rooms to accommodate the visitors, so everybody stayed up all night. The festival was held in a tobacco warehouse across the tracks from the center of town. The first night the Whites celebrated. They left all the decorations up, so Blacks moved in and celebrated the next night. We were well paid – $3000, the highest pay we received for a one-nighter.

The 1949 June German was something solid in a changing

scene. One got the idea everything was as it always had been and always would be, but as our bus headed out of Rocky Mount for Fort Worth, Texas, the next morning, I began to notice in towns we passed through, places we'd played in earlier years, that the ballrooms had become supermarkets, or bowling alleys, or roller rinks.

In Fort Worth we played a black dance at a ballroom in a building owned by a black lodge. In Wichita, Kansas, we played for another black lodge at a ballroom. At least these places were still open for dancing. Same with the the Rainbow Ballroom in Denver, and one in Brandon, Manitoba.

Traveling through South and North Dakota, I was amazed and thrilled at the sight of the wheat – miles and miles and miles of it. I wondered, "How can a farmer have hands to cut this wheat?" Combines, of course, were the answer, and students from agricultural colleges were sometimes brought in to operate them. I think of that when I read about shortages now. How can there be shortages in all this plenty?

We ended the tour at the Tune Town in St Louis. But I saw the handwriting on the wall. In fact, the year before I saw signs of the end of something. We were heading west again to open a new club in Los Angeles run by Joe Morris, owner of the Plantation Club where we'd done turnaway business in 1945. Morris had never forgotten it. He thought people would drop everything to come and hear Andy Kirk. He had even come to New York to plead with Joe Glaser to send us out to LA. I met Morris in Glaser's office. I listened to him: all he needed for his new club to take off was Andy Kirk. I decided to go out. My son Andy was playing tenor with me then. The write-ups in the papers were all about him because he was playing bop, and people had become bop indoctrinated.

Harry Truman became president while we were out there, and we were playing in a place where *we* were president and nothing happened. Los Angeles in 1948 was dead for big bands. All of a sudden darkness fell.

We went in the hole on our 1949 tour. Basie had cut down to a small band. Joe Glaser said, "Andy, do me a favor, cut down."

I said, "No, I'm not used to a small band sound." Into the early 1950s, even after I'd gotten a license to sell real-estate and began fooling around with that, I was still doing some gigs with the full band, made up of musicians living in the New York area. I still had records around, so clubs and organizations would call me for dates. And I still had Harry "Big Jim" Lawson on trumpet. He first joined me in 1926 and was the only original member who stuck the whole way.

One of our big numbers at that time was *The Whiffenpoof Song*. When we sang the line "We're little black sheep who have gone astray," we did it this way: "We're little" – hands over mouths – "sheep . . . " We never recorded it. I wish we had, but it was probably more effective visually. This came at about the end of the debutante scene. Was Brenda Frazier the last?

Then Blacks took it up. For 25 years I played the annual debutante ball sponsored by the National Council of Negro Women. We played many deb parties and dances and affairs for the social clubs, sportsmen's clubs, and organizations like the Railway Mail Clerks.

And I had met Ray Copeland, a fine young trumpet player. He was about 19 then. He knew several other young musicians around town and would tell me about them: Ted Kelly, a trombonist who had worked with Dizzy Gillespie; Billy Gordon, a tenor man; Wesley Landers, a drummer; Prince Babb, a bassist. Gradually we built a nucleus of young married musicians, all with day jobs – Kelly and Babb worked for the city, Gordon was with an accounting firm. They were eager to play but they had bought homes and were raising families, so beyond gigs in the surrounding areas they weren't interested in the road. For the past 20 years this nucleus of musicians Ray and I formed has been on hand to play Ruth Williams's annual dancing school concert at Carnegie or Avery Fisher Hall.

I began to get requests for small-group dates, but I didn't

have any arrangements for a small band. And I still thought I didn't like a small-band sound. Ray had the answer. "I have a dance book of arrangements for seven pieces," he told me. Through a booking office that handled bookings for me even after I was managing the Theresa Hotel here in Harlem, we got a job at a resort at White Roe Lake in the Catskills. We had fine singer with us, Leslie Scott. He was king in the Catskills until he took a Muslim name. He would bow to the East at intermission. Then he was dead with those Jewish people.

Mary and I went back to Kansas City in October 1975, just before we got started on this story, you remember, in connection with a documentary film on Kansas City jazz, sponsored by the Musicians' Foundation. They've moved the airport. It used to be in North Kansas City, across the river. It's 20 miles out now. That has changed the whole complexion of the city. Most people now live out in the country-club section.

We were looking for old Kansas City. We took a taxicab and I thought I was going to run out of money. The 12th Street area is all changed. The theaters and nightclubs have been torn down to make room for housing projects and new streets named after Mary Lou Williams, Charlie Parker, and other Kansas City jazz musicians. And 18th Street – oh, that's the saddest thing. It used to be very, very alive. The Streets Hotel, once the scene of Sunday matinee dances, wedding receptions and all sorts of social affairs, is now a vacant lot. Broken bricks just lying there. The Cherry Blossom, where Basie played, is no more. The house we stayed in directly across the street – I have a picture of little Andy in front of it – is gone, too.

One place from the old days is there, though. Matlaw's Haberdashery, on the southwest corner of 18th and Vine. All the musicians used to have accounts there. You could go in and buy and pay later. It has been enlarged and looks very neat and stands out there like a bright stone. Nothing around it is as clean. It's a desolate-looking spot. Ware's Barbershop is also still there, half a block away on 18th between Vine and

Paseo. That's where I used to get my hair cut. The *Kansas City Call* building on 18th is still in good shape, but stands by itself.

Part of 15th Street, a street that led from Kansas City to Independence, Missouri, Harry Truman's home, is now a throughway that traverses Kansas City. 15th and Paseo is a church now, but in its days as a dancing academy and ballroom, it was *the* place for Blacks. All the bands played there – Fats Waller, Duke Ellington, Fletcher Henderson, McKinney, and all the local bands. Union dances were held there and were always big events. We played 45 minutes or an hour non-stop, and had battles of music. The purpose was not to cut one another but to make money for the union so we could buy our own property. The Musicians' Foundation – that property – at 1823 Highland is still a neat, clean place.

The bands that made Kansas City the Jazz City are gone. But the music they recorded and the memories they made are not. They live.

Discography

compiled by Howard Rye

This discography includes all traced recordings on which Andy Kirk played or which were made by his bands, and recordings by small groups drawn from the bands. Band credits apply to subsequent sessions until an alternative credit is given, but it should be noted that from the late 1930s into the 1940s the credits "Andy Kirk and his Twelve Clouds of Joy," Andy Kirk and his Clouds of Joy" and "Andy Kirk and his Orchestra" were used interchangeably, possibly sometimes varying between different pressings of the same record, and it is unlikely that all variants have been accurately included.

As well as commercial recordings, both issued and unissued, surviving broadcasts, films, and transcription recordings (made for sale or lease to radio stations) have been included where known, but there may well be others.

In the case of issued small-group recordings, the precise instrumentation of each title has been determined, but this has not been possible in the case of recordings by the big band and it should not be assumed, for example, that all listed saxophones are heard on every title.

Vocalists and arrangers are indicated by initials following the title, except where the record credit is to the vocalist (in which case he or she sings on all titles from the session), and in the case of arrangements by Mary Lou Williams, which are asterisked. The arrangers of many items are unknown and it is likely that Mary Lou Williams, who was the band's principal arranger, made a larger contribution than is here indicated.

Original issues only are given. These are 78 r.p.m. 10" records unless presented in italics, in which case they are 12" LPs, or marked "16" ET", in which case they are transcription issues.

My thanks to Nigel Haslewood for assistance received.

Abbreviations

a	arranger
AFRS	Armed Forces Radio Service
as	alto saxophone
bar	baritone saxophone
bb	brass bass (tuba or sousaphone)
bj	banjo
bsx	bass saxophone
btb	bass trombone
cl	clarinet
d	drums
db	double bass
eg	electric guitar
ET	Electrical Transcription
g	guitar
ldr	leader
p	piano
t	trumpet
tb	trombone
ts	tenor saxophone
v	vocal
vb	vibraphone
vn	violin

Countries of Origin

All records listed are of United States origin, unless other-wise indicated:

Du Dutch   E British   J Japanese   Sd Swedish

Bibliography

The following works have been consulted:

Walter Bruyninckx: *60 Years of Recorded Jazz* (Mechelen, Belgium, 1978–80)

Jan Evensmo: *Jazz Solography Series*, vol. 7: *The Tenor Saxophones of Budd Johnson, Cecil Scott, Elmer Williams, Dick Wilson, 1927–1942* (Hosle, Norway, n.d.)

Galen Gart: *First Pressings: Rock History as Chronicled in*

Billboard Magazine, vol. 1: *1948–1950* (Milford, NH, 1986) (courtesy Tony Burke)

Jorgen Grunnet Jepsen: *Jazz Records 1942–1968* (Copenhagen, 1970) [vol.4c: J-Ki]

Rainer E. Lotz & Ulrich Neuert: *The AFRS "Jubilee" Transcription Programs: an Exploratory Discography* (Frankfurt, 1985)

Brian Rust: *Jazz Records 1897–1942* (5th revised and enlarged edition, Chigwell, Essex, n.d. [1984])

Harry Mackenzie: *AFRS Downbeat Series: a Working Draft* (Zephyrhills, FL, 1986)

Howard Rye: "The One that Got Away: George Morrison on Record," *Storyville 90* (1980), p. 218

Collectors Items and *Micrography* magazines

Use has been made of all available interviews with members of the band. It should be noted particularly that the name of Candy Johnson (ts) has been included in personnels for 1945–6 on the basis of his own testimony (to Hugues Panassié, *Bulletin du Hot Club de France*, no. 237 (1974), p.3), in place of that of Eddie Davis, whose tenure was much shorter than standard discographical sources currently imply.

1920
*c*26 March   New York City

Morrison's Jazz Orchestra

Leo Davis (t, as); Ed Caldwell (tb); Cuthbert Byrd (as); Andy Kirk (ts); George Morrison (vn, g); Jimmy Walker (p); Lee Morrison (bj); Alfredo Garcia (db); Eugene Montgomery (d)

49780-3	Pip-pip, Toot-toot, Goodbye-ee	Columbia rejected (12" master)
49781-3	So Long, Oo-long	Columbia rejected (12" master)

1920
*c*2 April   New York City

Same personnel as session of c26 March

79097-3	Royal Garden Blues	Columbia rejected

79098-3   I know why Introducing: Columbia rejected
                 My Cuban Dreams
At least one take of matrix 79097 still existed at Columbia in 1961.

1920
13 April   Camden, New Jersey

Same personnel as session of c26 March, except Garcia not present

                 Royal Garden Blues   Victor test recording,
                                                                      unissued
                 Jean   Victor test recording,
                                                                      unissued
Andy Kirk has no recollection of this session. George
Morrison recalls that it took place on a Friday, whereas the
date quoted above from Victor's files is a Tuesday.

1920
c22 April   New York City

Same personnel as session of c26 March

79098-6   I know why Introducing: Columbia A2945
                 My Cuban Dreams

1929
c7/8 November   Radio Station KMBC, Kansas City

Andy Kirk and his Twelve Clouds of Joy

*Gene Prince (t); Harry "Big Jim" Lawson (t, v); Allen Durham
(tb); John Harrington (cl, as); John Williams (as, bar); Lawrence
"Slim" Freeman (ts); Claude "Fiddler" Williams (vn, solo g); Mary
Lou Williams (p, a); William Dirvin (bj, g); Andy Kirk (bb, bsx,
ldr); Edward "Crackshot" McNeil (d)*

KC-591-A   Mess-a-Stomp*   Brunswick 4694

*John Harrington (cl); John Williams (bar); Claude "Fiddler"
Williams (vn, solo g); William Dirvin (g); Andy Kirk (bsx);
Edward "Crackshot" McNeil (d); Harry "Big Jim" Lawson (v)*

KC-592-A   Blue Clarinet Stomp* (HL, v)   Vocalion 3255
KC-592-B   Blue Clarinet Stomp* (HL, v)   Brunswick 4694

Same personnel as for KC-591-A; Billy Massey (v)

KC-593-A	Cloudy	Brunswick 4653
KC-594-	Casey Jones Special	Brunswick unissued
KC-595-	Casey Jones Special	Brunswick unissued
KC-596-A	Casey Jones Special (HL, BM, v)	Brunswick 4653
KC-597-	Casey Jones Special	Brunswick unissued

It is not certain which take of *Blue Clarinet Stomp* appears on which original issue. No information is available about the personnels of the unissued titles.

1929

*c*9 November   Radio Station KMBC, Kansas City

John Williams and his Memphis Stompers

Same personnel as for matrix KC-591-A

KC-600-A	Somepin' Slow and Low	Vocalion 1453
KC-601-A	Lotta Sax Appeal	Vocalion 1453

1929

*c*11 November   Radio Station KMBC, Kansas City

Andy Kirk and his Twelve Clouds of Joy

Same personnel as for matrix KC-591-A

KC-618-A	Corky Stomp*	Brunswick 4893
KC-619-A	Froggy Bottom	Brunswick 4893
KC-620-	Froggy Bottom	Brunswick unissued

1930

29 April   Chicago

Edgar "Puddin' Head" Battle, Harry "Big Jim" Lawson (t); Floyd "Stumpy" Brady (tb); John Harrington (cl, as); John Williams (as, bar); Lawrence "Slim" Freeman (ts); Claude "Fiddler" Williams (vn); Mary Lou Williams (p, a); William Dirvin (bj, g); Andy Kirk (bb, ldr); Ben Thigpen (d); Billy Massey (v)

C-4460-A	I lost my gal from Memphis (BM,v)	Brunswick 4803
C-4461-	I lost my gal from Memphis	Brunswick unissued
C-4462-A	Loose Ankles (BM, v)	Brunswick 4803
C-4463-	Loose Ankles	Brunswick unissued

1930
30 April   Chicago

Edgar "Puddin' Head" Battle, Harry "Big Jim" Lawson (t); Floyd "Stumpy" Brady (tb); John Harrington (cl, as); John Williams (as, bar); Lawrence "Slim" Freeman (ts); Claude "Fiddler" Williams (vn); Mary Lou Williams (p, a); William Dirvin (bj, g); Andy Kirk (bb, ldr); Ben Thigpen (d); Billy Massey (v)

C-4470-	Snag it	Brunswick 4878
C-4471-	Sweet and Hot	Brunswick 4878
C-4472-	Sweet and Hot	Brunswick unissued
C-4473	Mary's Idea	Brunswick 4863

1930
1 May   Chicago

Same personnel as session of 30 April

C-4480-	Once or Twice (BM, v)	Brunswick 4863

1930
15 July   Chicago

Seven Little Clouds of Joy

Harry "Big Jim" Lawson (t); Floyd "Stumpy" Brady (tb); John Williams (as); Mary Lou Williams (p); William Dirvin (bj); Andy Kirk (bb, ldr); Ben Thigpen (d)

C-6017-	Gettin' off a Mess	Brunswick 7180
C-6018-	You Rascal, You (BM, v)	Brunswick unissued

1930
30 September   Chicago

Andy Kirk and his Twelve Clouds of Joy
Same personnel as for 30 April 1930

C-6177-	Okay, Baby	Brunswick rejected
C-6178-	Dallas Blues (BM, v)	Brunswick rejected

1930
9 October   Chicago

Same personnel as for 30 April 1930

C-6430-A	Dallas Blues (BM, v)	Brunswick 6129

C-6431-	Travelin' that Rocky Road	Brunswick 4981
C-6432-	Honey, just for you (BM, v)	Brunswick 4981

Seven Little Clouds of Joy
Same personnel as for 30 April 1930 (notwithstanding the band credit)

C-6435-	You Rascal, You (BM, v)	Brunswick 7180

1930
15 December   New York City

Same personnel as for 30 April 1930; Dick Robertson (v)

E-35750-	Saturday (DR, v)	Brunswick 6027
E-35751-	Sophomore (DR, v)	Brunswick 6027

1931
2 March   Camden, New Jersey

Blanche Calloway and her Joy Boys
Harry "Big Jim" Lawson, Edgar "Puddin' Head" Battle (t); Clarence Smith (t,v); Floyd "Stumpy" Brady (tb); John Harrington (cl, as); John Williams (as, bar); Lawrence "Slim" Freeman (ts); Mary Lou Williams (p); William Dirvin (bj); Andy Kirk (bb); Ben Thigpen (d); Blanche Calloway, Billy Massey (v)

64068-1	Casey Jones Blues (BM, CS, v)	Victor 22640
64068-2	Casey Jones Blues (BM, CS, v)	*Gaps (Du) 160*
64069-1	There's rhythm in the river (BC, v)	*Gaps (Du) 160*
64069-2	There's rhythm in the river (BC, v)	Victor 22641
64070-1	I Need Lovin' (BC, v)	*Gaps (Du) 160*
64070-2	I Need Lovin' (BC, v)	Victor 22641
64070-3	I Need Lovin' (BC, v)	*Gaps (Du) 160*

1936
2 March   New York City

Andy Kirk and his Twelve Clouds of Joy
Harry "Big Jim" Lawson, Paul King, Earl Thomson (t); Ted Donnelly, Henry Wells (tb); John Harrington (cl, as, bar); John Williams (as, bar); Dick Wilson (ts); Claude "Fiddler" Williams

(vn); Mary Lou Williams (p, a); Ted Brinson (g); Booker Collins
(db); Ben Thigpen (d, v); Pha Terrell (v)

60852-A	Walkin' and Swingin'*	Columbia(E)	DB5023
60852-C	Walkin' and Swingin'*	Decca 809	
60853-A	Moten Swing*	Decca 853	
60854-A	Lotta Sax Appeal*	Decca 1046	

1936
3 March   New York City

Same personnel as for 2 March 1936

60861-A	Git (BT, ensemble, v)	Columbia(E)	DB5021
60861-B	Git (BT, ensemble, v)	Decca 931	
60861-C	Git (BT, ensemble, v)	Decca 931	
60862-A	All the jive is gone (PT, v)	Decca 744	

1936
4 March   New York City

Same personnel as for 2 March 1936

60865-A	Froggy Bottom (BT, v)	Decca 729
60865-B	Froggy Bottom (BT, v)	Decca 729
60866-A	Bearcat Shuffle	Decca 1046
60867-A	Steppin' Pretty	Decca 931

1936
7 March   New York City

Same personnel as for 2 March 1936

60874-A	Christopher Columbus	Decca 729
60876-A	Corky*	Decca 772

1936
11 March   New York City

Same personnel as for 2 March 1936

60886-A	I'se a muggin' (BT, v)	Decca 744	
60887-A	Until the real thing comes along (PT, v)	Columbia(E)	DB5004

1936
31 March   New York City

Same personnel as for 2 March 1936

60961-A	Puddin' Head Serenade	Columbia(E) DB5027

1936
2 April   New York City

Same personnel as for 2 March 1936

60972-A	Until the real thing comes along (PT, v)	Decca 809

1936
3 April   New York City

Same personnel as for 2 March 1936

60973-A	Blue Illusion (PT, v)	Decca 772
60974-A	Cloudy (PT, v)	Decca 1208

1936
7 April   New York City

Same personnel as for 2 March 1936

61003-A	Give her a pint (and she'll tell it all) (PT, v)	Decca 853

1936
10 April   New York City

Same personnel as for 2 March 1936

60961-C	Puddin' Head Serenade	Decca 1208

1936
9 December   New York City

Same personnel as for 2 March 1936; Harry Mills (v)

61463-A	Fifty-Second Street (HM, ensemble, v)	Decca 1146
61464-A	The lady who swings the band (HM, v)	Decca 1085
61465-A	What will I tell my heart? (PT, v)	Decca 1085
61466-B	Dedicated to You (PT, v)	Decca 1146

1937
29 January   Trianon Ballroom, Cleveland, Ohio

Probably same personnel as for 2 March 1936

Theme (Until the real thing comes along)	unissued
You turned the tables on me	unissued
Never slept a wink last night	*Jazz Society (Sd) AA503*
Goodnight my Love	unissued
You do the darnedest things	unissued
Spring Holiday	unissued
When I'm with you	unissued
Make Believe Ballroom	*Jazz Society (Sd) AA503*
Sepia Jazz	*Jazz Society (Sd) AA503*
Gypsy	unissued
Clouds	unissued
Theme (Until the real thing comes along)	unissued

1937
30 January   Trianon Ballroom, Cleveland, Ohio

Probably same personnel as for 2 March 1936

Theme (Until the real thing comes along)	unissued
You're Slightly Terrific	*Jazz Society (Sd) AA503*
Yours Truly	*Jazz Society (Sd) AA503*
Trust in Me (PT, v)	*Jazz Society (Sd) AA503*
All the jive is gone	*Jazz Society (Sd) AA503*
Dear Old Southland	*Jazz Society (Sd) AA503*
In the chapel in the moonlight	unissued
Theme (Until the real thing comes along)	unissued

1937
5 February   Trianon Ballroom, Cleveland, Ohio

Probably same personnel as for 2 March 1936

Theme (Until the real thing comes along)	unissued
Honeysuckle Rose	unissued
There's Frost on the Moon	unissued
Medley (PT, v) (*see footnote*)	*Jazz Society (Sd) AA503*
Walkin' and Swingin'	unissued

Dedicated to You	unissued
Oh say can you swing	unissued
King Porter Stomp	unissued
Liza	unissued
Theme (Until the real thing comes along)	unissued

The *Medley* comprises *Boo Hoo/One, two, button your shoe/Trouble don't like Music/One in a Million*

1937
6 February   Trianon Ballroom, Cleveland, Ohio

Probably same personnel as for 2 March 1936

Theme (Until the real thing comes along)	*Jazz Society (Sd) AA503*
Swingtime in the Rockies	*Jazz Society (Sd) AA503*
Froggy Bottom	*Jazz Society (Sd) AA503*
What will I tell my heart (PT, v)	*Jazz Society (Sd) AA503*
Moten Swing	*Jazz Society (Sd) AA503*
I love you from coast to coast	*Jazz Society (Sd) AA503*
Organ Grinder's Swing (PT, v)	*Jazz Society (Sd) AA503*
Theme (Until the real thing comes along	*Jazz Society (Sd) AA503*

1937
15 February   New York City

Harry "Big Jim" Lawson, Paul King, Earl Thomson (t); Ted Donnelly (tb); Henry Wells (tb, v); John Harrington (cl, as, bar); John Williams (as, bar); Earl Miller (as); Dick Wilson (ts); Mary Lou Williams (p, a); Ted Brinson (g); Booker Collins (db); Ben Thigpen (d); Pha Terrell (v)

61598-A	Wednesday Night Hop	Decca 1303
61958-?	Wednesday Night Hop	*Decca DL9232*
61599-A	Skies are Blue (PT, v)	Decca 1349
61950-B	Downstream (PT, v)	Decca 1531
61951-A	In the Groove	Decca 1261

Wednesday Night Hop was arranged by Leslie Johnakins.

1937
17 April   New York City

Same personnel as for 15 February 1937

62133-A	Worried over you (PT, v)	Decca 1303
62134-B	Foolin' Myself (PT, v)	Decca 1261
62135-A	I'm glad for your sake (But I'm sorry for mine) (PT, v)	Decca 1531
62136-A	I'll Get Along Somehow (PT, v)	Decca 1349

1937
26 July   New York City

Same personnel as for 15 February 1937

62446-A	A Mellow Bit of Rhythm*	Decca 1579
62447-A	In my Wildest Dreams (PT, v)	Decca 1579
62448-A	Better Luck Next Time (PT, v)	Decca 1422
62449-A	With Love in my Heart (PT, v)	Decca 1477

1937
27 July   New York City

Same personnel as for 15 February 1937

62453-B	What's Mine is Yours (PT, v)	Decca 1827
62454-A	Why can't we do it again? (HW, v)	Decca 1477
62455-A	The Key to my Heart (PT, v)	Decca 1710
62456-A	I want to be a gypsy (PT, v)	Decca 1422

1937
13 December   New York City

Harry "Big Jim" Lawson, Clarence Trice, Earl Thomson (t); Ted Donnelly (tb); Henry Wells (tb, v); John Harrington (cl, as, bar); John Williams (as, bar); Earl Miller (as); Dick Wilson (ts); Mary Lou Williams (p, a); Ted Brinson (g); Booker Collins (db); Ben Thigpen (d, v); Pha Terrell (v)

62872-A	Lover, come back to me (PT, v)	Decca 1663
62873-A	Poor Butterfly (PT, v)	Decca 1663
62874-A	The Big Dipper	Decca 1606
62875-A	Bear Down*	Decca 1606

1938
8 February   New York City

Same personnel as for 13 December 1937

| 63255-A | I Surrender, Dear (PT, v) | Decca 1916 |

63256-A	Twinklin'	Decca 2483
63257-A	It Must be True (PT, v)	Decca 1827
63258-A	I'll Get by (HW, v)	Decca 1916
63259-A	Little Joe from Chicago (ensemble, v)*	Decca 1710

1938
9 September   New York City

Rodney Sturgis

Rodney Sturgis (v); acc. unknown (t); Mary Lou Williams (p); Ted Brinson (g); Booker Collins (db); Ben Thigpen (d); unknown band members (v)

| 64612-A | The gal that wrecked my life | Decca 7550 |

Andy Kirk and his Twelve Clouds of Joy

Same personnel as for 13 December 1937

64613-A	Bless You, my Dear (PT, v)	Decca 2204
64614-A	How can we be wrong? (PT, v)	Decca 2081
64615-A	Mess-a Stomp*	Decca 2204

1938
12 September   New York City

Same personnel as for 13 December 1937

64642-A	Toadie Toddle (BT, v)	Decca 2127
64643-A	I won't tell a soul (I love you) (PT, v)	Decca 2127
64644-A	What Would People Say? (PT, v)	Decca 2277
64645-A	How much do you mean to me? (PT, v)	Decca 2081

1938
24 October   New York City

Same personnel as for 13 December 1937

64694-A	Jump Jack Jump	Decca 2226
64695-A	Breeze (PT, v)	Decca 2261
64696-A	Ghost of Love (PT, v)	Decca 2226
64697-A	What a Life (PT, v)	Decca 2617

1938
25 October   New York City

Same personnel as for 13 September 1937

| 64698-A | Sittin' Around and Dreamin' (PT, v) | Decca 2261 |
| 64699-A | What's your Story, Morning Glory? (PT, v) | Decca 3306 |

1938
5 December   New York City

Same personnel as for 13 September 1937; O'Neill Spencer (v)

64777-A	Honey (PT, v)	Decca 2326
64778-A	September in the Rain (PT, v)	Decca 2617
64779-A	Clouds (PT, v)	Decca 2570
64780-A	Julius Caesar (O'NS, v)	Decca 2383
64781-A	Dunkin' a Doughnut	Decca 2723

1938
6 December   New York City

Same personnel as for 13 September 1937

64782-A	Goodbye (PT, v)	Decca 2570
64783-A	Mary's Idea*	Decca 2326
64784-A	But it didn't mean a thing (PT, v)	Decca 2277
64785-A	Say it Again (PT, v)	Decca 2774

1939
16 March   New York City

Harry "Big Jim" Lawson, Clarence Trice, Earl Thomson (t); Ted Donnelly, Henry Wells (tb); John Harrington (cl, as, bar); Earl "Buddy" Miller (as); Don Byas, Dick Wilson (ts); Mary Lou Williams (p, a); Floyd "Wonderful" Smith (g, eg); Booker Collins (db); Ben Thigpen (d); June Richmond, Pha Terrell (v)

65188-A	You set me on fire (PT, v)	Decca 2383
65189-A	I'll never learn (PT, v)	Decca 2510
65190-A	Close to Five	Decca 2407
65191-A	Floyd's Guitar Blues*	Decca 2483

1939
23 March   New York City

Same personnel as for 16 March 1939

65249-A	Then I'll be Happy (JR, v)	Decca 2723
65250-A	S'posin' (PT, v)	Decca 2510
65251-A	I'll Never Fail You (PT, v)	Decca 2407
65252-A	Why don't I get wise to myself? (PT, v)	Decca 2774

1939
15 November   New York City

Same personnel as for 16 March 1939

66877-A	I'm getting nowhere with you (PT, v)	Decca 2957
66878-A	I don't stand a ghost of a chance (PT, v)	Decca 2915
66879-A	Please don't talk about me when I'm gone (JR, v)	Decca 3033
66880-A	Big Jim Blues*	Decca 2915

1940
2 January   New York City

Harry "Big Jim" Lawson, Clarence Trice, Earl Thomson (t); Ted Donnelly, Jim Robinson (tb); John Harrington (cl, as, bar); Earl "Buddy" Miller (as); Don Byas, Dick Wilson (ts); Mary Lou Williams (p, a); Floyd "Wonderful" Smith (g, eg); Booker Collins (db); Ben Thigpen (d); June Richmond, Pha Terrell (v)

67010-A	Wham (Wham-re-bop-boom-bam) (JR, v)	Decca 2962
67010-B	Wham (Wham-re-bop-boom-bam) (JR, v)	Decca 2962
67011-A	Love is the Thing (PT, v)	Decca 2962
67012-A	Why go on pretending? (PT, v)	Decca 3033
67013-A	It always will be you (JR, v)	Decca 2957

1940
26 January   New York City

Six Men and a Girl

Earl Thomson (t); Earl "Buddy" Miller (cl-1, as-2); Dick Wilson (ts); Mary Lou Williams (p); Floyd "Wonderful" Smith (g); Booker Collins (db); Ben Thigpen (d)

US-1316-1	Mary Lou Williams Blues	Varsity 8193
	−1, 2	
US-1317-1	Tea for Two −2	Varsity 8193
US-1318-1	Scratchin' the Gravel −2	Varsity 8190
US-1319-1	Zonky −1	Varsity 8190

1940
20 March   Cotton Club, New York City

Andy Kirk & his Clouds of Joy

Harry "Big Jim" Lawson, Harold "Shorty" Baker, Clarence Trice (t); Ted Donnelly, Fred Robinson (tb); Rudy Powell, John Harrington (cl, as); Edward Inge (cl, ts); Dick Wilson (ts); Mary Lou Williams (p, a); Floyd "Wonderful" Smith (g, eg); Booker Collins (db); Ben Thigpen (d); June Richmond, Pha Terrell (v)

| The Sheik of Araby | unissued |
| Cherokee | unissued |

1940
5 May   Cotton Club, New York City

Personnel as for 20 March 1940

| The Sheik of Araby | *Everybody's EV3006* |
| Marcheta | *Everybody's EV3006* |

1940
6 May   Cotton Club, New York City

Personnel as for 20 March 1940

| The Riff | *Everbody's EV3006* |

1940
24 May   Cotton Club, New York City

Personnel as for 20 March 1940

| The Riff | unissued |

1940
25 June   New York City

Andy Kirk and his Twelve Clouds of Joy

Personnel as for 20 March 1940

67893-A	Fine and Mellow (JR, v)	Decca 3282
67894-A	Scratching in the Gravel	Decca 3293
67895-A	Fifteen Minutes Intermission (JR, v)	Decca 3282
67896-A	Take Those Blues Away (JR, v)	Decca 3293

1940
8 July   New York City

Personnel as for 20 March 1940

67917-A	Now I lay me down to dream (PT, v)	Decca 3306
67918-A	No Greater Love (PT, v)	Decca 3350
67919-A	Midnight Stroll (JR, v)	Decca 3350
67920-A	Little Miss	Decca 3491

1940
7 November   New York City

Harry "Big Jim" Lawson, Harold "Shorty" Baker, Clarence Trice (t); Ted Donnelly (tb); Henry Wells (tb, v); Rudy Powell, John Harrington (cl, as); Edward Inge (cl, ts); Dick Wilson (ts); Mary Lou Williams (p, a); Floyd "Wonderful" Smith (g, eg); Booker Collins (db); Ben Thigpen (d); June Richmond (v)

68317-A	The Count	Decca 18123
68318-A	Twelfth Street Rag	Decca 18123
68319-A	When I saw you (HW, v)	Decca 3491

1940
18 November   New York City

Andy Kirk and his Clouds of Joy
Personnel as for 7 November 1940

68363-A	If I feel this way tomorrow (HW, v)	Decca 3582
68364-A	Or have I (HW, v)	Decca 3582

Mary Lou Williams and her Kansas City Seven
Harold "Shorty" Baker (t); Ted Donnelly (tb); Edward Inge (cl, a); Dick Wilson (ts); Mary Lou Williams (p); Booker Collins (db); Ben Thigpen (d)

| 68365-A | Baby Dear | Decca 18122 |
| 68366-A | Harmony Blues | Decca 18122 |

1941
3 January New York City

Andy Kirk and his Twelve Clouds of Joy

Same personnel as for 7 November 1940

68546-A	Cuban Boogie Woogie (JR, v)	Decca 3663
68547-A	A dream dropped in (HW, v)	Decca 3619
68548-A	Is it a Sin (Loving You)? (HW, v)	Decca 3619
68549-A	Ring dem Bells	Decca 3663

1941
17 July New York City

Andy Kirk and his Clouds of Joy

Harry "Big Jim" Lawson, Harold "Shorty" Baker, Clarence Trice (t); Ted Donnelly (tb); Henry Wells (tb, v); John Harrington (cl, as); Earl "Buddy" Miller (as); Edward Inge (cl, ts); Dick Wilson (ts); Mary Lou Williams (p, a); Floyd "Wonderful" Smith (g, eg); Booker Collins (db); Ben Thigpen (d); June Richmond (v)

69519-A	Big Time Crip (ensemble, v)	Decca 4042
69520-B	47th Street Jive (JR, v)	Decca 4042
69521-A	I'm Misunderstood (HW, v)	Decca 4141
69522-A	No Answer (HW, v)	Decca 4141

1942
14 July New York City

Andy Kirk and his Clouds of Joy

Johnny Burris, Harry "Big Jim" Lawson (t); Howard McGhee (t, a); Ted Donnelly, Milton Robinson (tb); John Harrington (cl, as); Ben Smith (as); Edward Inge (cl, ts); Al Sears (ts); Kenny Kersey (p, a); Floyd "Wonderful" Smith (g, eg); Booker Collins (db); Ben Thigpen (d); June Richmond (v)

71050-A	Hey Lawdy Mama (JR, v)	Decca 4405
71051-A	Boogie Woogie Cocktail (KK, a)	Decca 4381
71052-A	Ride on, ride on (JR, v)	Decca 4436
71053-A	McGhee Special (HMcG, a)	Decca 4405

1942

29 July   New York City

Same personnel as for 14 July 1942

71239-A	Worried Life Blues (FS, v)	Decca 4381
71240-A	Take it and git it (ensemble, v)	Decca 4366
71241-A	Hip Hip Hooray (JR, v)	Decca 4366
71242-B	Unlucky Blues (JR, v)	Decca 4436

1943

cNovember   Hollywood, California

Andy Kirk and his Orchestra

*Probable personnel: Cliff Haughton, Harry "Big Jim" Lawson,
Howard McGhee, Fats Navarro, Art Capeheart (t); Joe Baird,
Wayman Richardson, Bob Murray, Ted Donnelly (tb); John
Harrington (cl, as, ts); Ben Smith, Reuben Phillips (as); J.D. King,
Jimmy Forrest (ts); Eddie Loving (bar); Johnny Young (p); Booker
Collins (db); Ben Thigpen (d); June Richmond (v)*

(I found my love in) Avalon	AFRS Jubilee #54 (16"ET)
Wednesday Night Hop	AFRS Jubilee #54
If that's the way you want it (JR, v)	AFRS Jubilee #54
Hit that Jive, Jack (JR, v)	AFRS Jubilee #54
Seven Come Eleven	AFRS Jubilee #54

1943

3 December   New York City

*Harry "Big Jim" Lawson, Art Capeheart, Fats Navarro, Howard
McGhee (t); Joe Baird, Wayman Richardson, Bob Murray, Ted
Donnelly (tb); Ben Smith, Reuben Phillips (as); John Harrington,
Jimmy Forrest, J. D. King (ts); Eddie Loving (bar); Johnny Young
(p); Booker Collins (db); Ben Thigpen (d); June Richmond (v)*

71535-	Shorty Boo	*MCA(J) MCA3151*
71536-	Fare thee well, honey (JR, v)	Decca 4449
71537-	Baby don't you tell me no lie (JR, v)	Decca 4449
71538-	Things 'bout comin' my way	Decca unissued

1944

cFebruary   Hollywood, California

Probably same personnel as for cNovember 1943; Timmie Rogers,
Andy Kirk (v); Howard McGhee (a)

Hallelujah Heaven	AFRS Jubilee #66 (16"ET)
Get up Mule (JR, v)	AFRS Jubilee #66
Speak Low	AFRS Jubilee #66
Paradise Alley	AFRS Jubilee #66
Wednesday Night Hop	AFRS Jubilee #67 (16"ET)
McGhee Special (HMcG, a)	AFRS Jubilee #67
Knock me a kiss (if you can't smile and say yes) (TR, v)	AFRS Jubilee #67
47th Street Jive (JR, AK, v)	AFRS Jubilee #67
Peeping through the keyhole (incomplete)	AFRS Jubilee #67

Additional titles from this period are on (16"ET) AFRS
Jubilee #68, but details are not available.

1944

cMarch   unknown location

Probably same personnel as for cFebruary 1944

Ride on	*AFRS Downbeat #74 (16" ET)*
My heart tells me (JR, v)	*AFRS Downbeat #74 (16" ET)*
Paradise Valley	*AFRS Downbeat #74 (16" ET)*
I couldn't sleep a wink last night	*AFRS Downbeat #74 (16" ET)*
Wednesday Night Hop	*AFRS Downbeat #74 (16" ET)*
My Ideal (JR, v)	*AFRS Downbeat #74 (16" ET)*
Blue Skies	*AFRS Downbeat #74 (16" ET)*
Get Out, Mule (JR, v)	*AFRS Downbeat #74 (16" ET)*
Take it and git	*AFRS Downbeat #74 (16" ET)*

Some of the above titles may be identical to the versions on the other
AFRS ETs.

1944

unknown date   unknown source (possibly from AFRS)

Harry "Big Jim" Lawson, Fats Navarro, Howard McGhee, Art
Capeheart (t); Bob Murray, Joe Baird, Wayman Richardson, Ted
Donnelly (tb); Ben Smith (as); John Harrington, Jimmy Forrest, J.
D. King (ts); Eddie Loving (bar); Johnny Young (p); Booker Collins
(db); Ben Thigpen (d); June Richmond (v)

Roll 'em	*Hindsight HSR227*
Together	*Hindsight HSR227*

Hey Lordy Mama (JR, v)	*Hindsight HSR227*
920 Special	*Hindsight HSR227*
St Louis Blues	*Hindsight HSR227*
Seven Come Eleven	*Hindsight HSR227*
47th Street Jive (JR, v)	*Hindsight HSR227*
Boo Wah	*Hindsight HSR227*
Avalon	*Hindsight HSR227*

1944

19 December   New York City

Harry "Big Jim" Lawson, Fats Navarro, Art Capeheart, unknown (t); Bob Murray, Joe Baird, Wayman Richardson (tb); Ben Smith (as); John Harrington, Jimmy Forrest, J. D. King (ts); Eddie Loving (bar); Johnny Young (p); Lavern Baker (db); Ben Thigpen (d)

72644-	Apollo Groove	Decca unissued
72645-	So Blue	Decca unissued
72646-	Hippy Dippy	*MCA(J) MCA3151*
72647-	If that's the way you want it	Decca unissued

1945

cMay   Hollywood, California

Probable personnel: Harry "Big Jim" Lawson, John Lynch, Talib Dawood, Claude Dunson (t); Milton Robinson, Wayman Richardson, Bob Murray (tb); Joe Evans (as); Reuben Phillips (as, cl); Jimmy Forrest, Eddie Davis (ts); Johnny Taylor (bar); Hank Jones (p); Floyd "Wonderful" Smith (g); Lavern Baker (db); Ben Thigpen (d); Gwynn Tine, June Richmond, Danny Kaye, Andy Kirk, Lena Horne (v)

Roll 'em	AFRS Jubilee #133 (16"ET)
Ain't got nothin' but the blues (LH, v)	AFRS Jubilee #133
As long as I live (LH, v)	AFRS Jubilee #133
Avalon	AFRS Jubilee #133
9.20 Special	AFRS Jubilee #134 (16"ET)
Don't talk about me when I'm gone (GT, v)	AFRS Jubilee #134
Seven Come Eleven	AFRS Jubilee #134
Together	AFRS Jubilee #134
Knick Knack (Nick Nack)	AFRS Jubilee #135 (16"ET)

47th Street Jive (JR, AK, v)	AFRS Jubilee #135
Comedy Skit (DK, v)	AFRS Jubilee #135
Minnie the Moocher (DK, audience, v)	AFRS Jubilee #135
Hey, Lawdy Mama (JR, v)	AFRS Jubilee #135

1945
27 November   New York City

Harry "Big Jim" Lawson, Claude Dunson, Talib Dawood, John Lynch (t); Milton Robinson, Henry Wells, Bob Murray, Wayman Richardson (tb); Joe Evans, Reuben Phillips (as); Jimmy Forrest, Floyd "Candy" Johnson (ts); Johnny Taylor (bar); Hank Jones (p); Floyd "Wonderful" Smith (g); Lavern Baker (db); Ben Thigpen (d); The Jubalaires (v)

73161-	Get Together with the Lord (T.Js, v)	Decca 18782
73162-	I Know (T.Js, v)	Decca 18782
73163-	Soothe Me	Decca unissued

1946
3 January   *New York City*

Harry "Big Jim" Lawson, Claude Dunson, John Lynch, Fats Navarro (t); Milton Robinson, Henry Wells, Bob Murray, Wayman Richardson (tb); Joe Evans, Reuben Phillips (as); Jimmy Forrest, Floyd "Candy" Johnson (ts); John Porter (bar); Hank Jones (p); Floyd "Wonderful" Smith (g); Al Hall (db); Ben Thigpen (d); Beverley White, Bea Booze, Billy Daniels (v)

73264-	He's my Baby (BW, v)	Decca 23870
73265-	Alabama Bound (BB, v)	Decca 48073
73266-	Soothe Me (BD, v)	Decca 23870
73867-	Doggin' Man Blues	Decca 48073

1946
23 May   New York City

Probably similar personnel to 3 January 1946, except unknown (t) replaces Navarro; The Jubalaires (v)

73590-	I don't know what I'd do without you	Decca 18916
73591-	I'm so lonesome I could cry (T.Js, v)	Decca 18916

1946
2 December   New York City

Fip Ricard, Clarence Trice, John Lynch, unknown (t); Milton Robinson, Henry Wells, Bob Murray, Wayman Richardson (tb); Joe Evans, Reuben Phillips (as); Jimmy Forrest, Floyd "Candy" Johnson (ts); John Porter (bar); Hank Jones (p); Floyd "Wonderful" Smith (g); Al Hall (db); Ben Thigpen (d); Joe Williams (v)

73751-	Now you tell me	Decca 23959
73752-	Louella (JW, v)	Decca 23959
73753-	So Soon	Decca 24139
73754-	I'm falling for you (JW, v)	Decca 24139

1947
unknown date   Pathé Studios, East 116th Street, New York City

Probably similar personnel to last session

Gator Serenade	unissued
Apollo Groove	unissued
Basie Boogie	unissued

These titles are from the soundtrack of the All American News film *Killer Diller*. There are probably additional numbers by Kirk's band in the film.

1949
cApril/May   New York City

Andy Kirk and his Clouds of Joy

Unknown personnel

| Drinkin' Wine, Spo-dee-o-dee, Drinkin' Wine | Vocalion 55010 |
| Little Girl | Vocalion 55010 |

This record was reviewed in the June 1949 issue of *Billboard*.

1954
31 March   New York City

Unknown personnel, except: H-Bomb Ferguson, Mel Moore (v)

| Hole in the Wall (H-BF, v) | Decca 29167 |
| Mind if I remind you (MM, v) | Decca 29167 |

1956

4 March   New York City

Andy Kirk and his Clouds of Joy

Conte Candoli, Ray Copeland, Bernie Glow, Joe Newman (t);
Jimmy Cleveland, Frank Rehak, Chauncey Welsh (tb); Tom
Mitchell (btb); Sam Marowitz, Hal McKusick (as); Al Cohn, Ed
Wasserman (ts); Al Epstein (bar); Ken Kersey (p); Freddie Green
(g); Milt Hinton (db); Osie Johnson (d, v); Manny Albam, Ernie
Wilkins (a)

G2-JB-2510	Scratchin' in the Gravel	*RCA-Victor LPM1302*
G2-JB-2511	Wednesday Night Hop	*RCA-Victor LPM1302*
G2-JB-2512	Froggy Bottom (OJ, v)	*RCA-Victor LPM1302*
G2-JB-2513	A Mellow Bit of Rhythm	*RCA-Victor LPM1302*
G2-JB-2514	Walkin' and Swingin'	*RCA-Victor LPM1302*
G2-JB-2515	Take it and git	*RCA-Victor LPM1302*
G2-JB-2516	Boogie Woogie Cocktail	*RCA-Victor LPM1302*
G2-JB-2517-2	Cloudy	RCA-Victor rejected

1956

12 March   New York City

Conte Candoli, Ray Copeland, Bernie Glow, Ernie Royal (t); Jimmy
Cleveland, Fred Ohms, Chauncey Welsh (tb); Tom Mitchell (btb);
Sam Marowitz, Hal McKusick (as); Al Cohn, Ed Wasserman (ts);
Al Epstein (bar); Marty Wilson (vb); Moe Wechler (p); Jimmy
Raney (g); Buddy Jones (db); Osie Johnson (d)

G2-JB-2517-7	Cloudy	*RCA-Victor LPM1302*
G2-JB-2855	Toadie Toddle	*RCA-Victor LPM1302*
G2-JB-2856	Little Joe from Chicago	*RCA-Victor LPM1302*
G2-JB-2857	Hey Lawdy Mama	*RCA-Victor LPM1302*
G2-JB-2858	McGhee Special	*RCA-Victor LPM1302*

Index

AK Blues, 23
Alexander, Willard, 87
Alice Blue Gown, 62
Allen, Henry "Tin Can," 48
Allen, Jap, 65
Albert, Don, 88
Andrews, Jessie, 44
Armstrong, Louis, 54, 84
Atlanta
   City Auditorium, 92
   Jewish Progressive Club, 90

Babb, Prince, 117
Bailey, Mildred, 114
Baltimore
   Astoria, 84
Banion, Arcee [cousin], 5, 7, 8, 9, 34
Banion, Celeste [cousin], 5, 7
Banion, Jimmy [cousin], 5, 6, 8, 9,
   13–15, 58
Banion, Mary [aunt], 4, 5, 6, 8,
   19–20, 30, 114–15
Banks, Paul, 65
Basie, Count, 65, 85, 117
Battle, Edgar, 2
Beer Barrell Polka, 111
Benson, Flip, 59
Bergen, Freddy, 72
Better Luck Next Time, 87
Biagini, Hank, 73
Billboard, 53
Birmingham, Alabama
   Pickwick Club, 97
Blind Boone, 29
Blue Clarinet Stomp, 71
Boogie Woogie Cocktail, 111
Bowl of Pansies, A, 44
Brady, Stumpy, 2

Brooks, Harvey, 48
Brymn, Tim, 44
Buchanan, Jimmy, 87
Bushkin, Joe, 107

Cahn, Sammy, 85
Calloway, Blanche, 103
Calloway, Cab, 60, 61
Calloway, Harriet, 85
Casa Loma Orchestra, 72, 73
Casey Jones, 62, 71
Chapman, Saul, 85
Chicago
   Vendome Theater, 54
   Warwick Hall, 54
Christopher Columbus, 84
Clouds, 91
Cobb, Arnett, 88
Colston, Jimmy [brother-in-law],
   16, 68
Colston, Mary [wife], 16, 24, 31–2,
   44, 45, 49, 51, 52, 68, 82, 114
Cooke, Charlie, 54
Coon-Sanders Orchestra, 57; see
   also Sanders, Joe
Copeland, Ray, 117–18
Corky, 73
Corrigan, Hugh, 113
Coy, Happy Gene, 46
Crowe, George, 84

Dallas
   North Dallas Club, 55
   Ozarks Club, 54
Dallas Blues, 71
Darktown Strutters' Ball, 110
Davis, Eddie "Lockjaw," 111
Davis, Joe, 95

Davis, Leo, 44, 47, 51
Dedicated to you, 86
Deep in the Heart of Texas, 101
Denver
   The Boulevard, 52
   Lakeside Amusement Park,
      45, 46
   Moonlight Ranch, 52–3
   Rock Rest, 49
Donnelly, Ted, 2
Dorsey, Jimmy, 110
Duncan, Harold, 83, 87
Durham, Allen, 59, 62

Eberly, Bob, 110
Ellington, Duke, 119

Fifty-Second Street, 87
Forrest, Jimmy, 109–10
Froggy Bottom, 71

Gifford, Gene, 73
Git, 86
Glaser, Joe, 84, 87, 93–4, 110, 113,
   116, 117
Gordon, Billy, 117
Gorman, Ross, 46
Grant, Lester, 52

Hall, Stewart, 52
Hammond, John, 87
Harrington, John, 59
Harris, Charlie, 54
Hart, Clyde, 65
Hayes, Thaymon, 65
Hazlitt, Chet, 46
Henderson, Fletcher, 66–7, 85, 104,
   119
Hereford, Leon, 48
Hey Lawdy, Mama, 110
Hill, Alex, 85
Hines, Earl, 54
Holder, Terrence, 54, 55, 56, 58, 59,
   64
Howard, Paul, 48

I went to the gypsy, 87

Jackson, Marion, 70, 72
Jacquet, Illinois, 88
Johnson, Budd, 55
Johnson, Keg, 55
Johnson, Pete, 68
Jones, Hank, 111
Jones, Jo, 89
June, 46
Junior, Frank, Jr, 41, 51, 52

Kansas City
   Fairyland Park, 83, 86, 87
   Piney Brown's, 68
   Pla-Mor, 60, 61, 62, 63, 66, 70
   Vanity Fair, 78
   Winwood Beach Amusement
      Park, 81
Kapp, Jack, 84–5
Kelly, Ted, 117
Kersey, Ken, 111
Killer Diller, 114
King, J. D., 109–10
Kirk, Andy [son], 68, 75, 82, 116
Kirk, Charles [father], 4
Kirk, Dellah [mother], 4, 8
Kirk, Mary; see Colston, Mary
Kiss me again, 62

Lady who swings the band, 86–7
Lakeland, Florida
   Lakeland Country Club, 92
Landers, Wesley, 117
Lawson, Harry "Big Jim," 62, 117
Lee, George E., 59–60, 65, 75,
   79–80
Lee, Julia, 60
Leonard, Harlan, 65
Let me call you sweetheart, 57
Lombardo, Guy, 57
Los Angeles
   Plantation Club, 110
Love, Clarence, 65
Lovely to look at, 1
Loving, Ed, 109–10
Lullaby of the Leaves, 83, 102
Lunceford, Jimmie, 49, 98, 108

McDaniel, Hattie, 47–8
McGhee, Howard, 109
McKinney's Cotton Pickers, 66, 78, 119
McShann, Jay, 65
Mary's Idea, 71
Massey, Billy, 61, 62
Mellow Bit of Rhythm, A, 50
Mess-a-stomp, 71
Minor, Dan, 55
Montgomery, Gene, 51
Morris, Joe, 116
Morrison, George, 24, 29, 38, 43–4, 45, 46, 47, 50, 94
Morton, Jelly Roll, 46–7
Morton, Norwell "Flutes," 54
Moten, Bennie, 50, 65, 71
My Buddy, 53

Navarro, Fats, 111
New York
    Alhambra Theater, 104–5
    Apollo Theater, 104–5, 111
    Arcadia Ballroom, 113
    Carleton Terrace, 44
    Golden Gate Ballroom, 101
    Kansas City Barbecue, 114
    Manhattan Center, 110
    Roseland Ballroom, 71–2
    Savoy Ballroom, 77, 104
Norvo, Red, 114

O'Connell, Helen, 110
Oklahoma City
    Blossom Heath, 82–3
    Winter Garden, 57
Opelousas, Louisiana
    The Pines, 93
Over There, 53

Page, Walter, 65
Parker, Charlie, 80, 118
Pettis, Jack, 45
Philadelphia
    Pearl Theater, 103
Pittman, Booker, 55

Poor Butterfly, 36, 86
Prince, Gene, 59

Quality Four, 48

Randolph, Irving "Mousie," 83–4
Rath, Franz, 40
Redman, Don, 66, 73, 84, 97
Richmond, June, 110–11
Ross, Theodore, 59

St Louis
    Tune Town Ballroom, 105
St Louis Blues, 101
Sanders, Joe, 77; see also Coon-Sanders Orchestra
Scoggins, Chick, 60
Scott, Leslie, 118
Sharpe, Billy, 98–9, 106, 109
Shaw, Milt, 72
Sissle, Noble, 104
Slave Song, A, 85
Smith, Floyd, 112
Smith, Willie, 25
Snag it, 71
Society Syncopators, 54

Tate, Erskine, 54
Teagarden, Jack, 57
Terrell, Pha, 1, 83–4, 102–3
Thigpen, Ben, 1, 96–7, 103
Trent, Alphonso, 54, 94
Tulsa
    Crystal City Park, 59
Turner, Joe, 68
Twenty Years on Wheels, 2

Until the real thing comes along, 86, 87, 88, 104, 110

Walder, Woodie, 50
Wall, Alvin "Fats," 50, 53, 54, 56, 58–9
Waller, Fats, 85, 119
Washington, Jackie, 89
Webster, Ben, 1, 65

Welk, Lawrence, 75
Wells, Henry, 108
West, Desdemona, 44, 51
Whalen, Tom, 104
Wham, 91
What'll I tell my heart, 86
When the saints go marching in, 95
Whiffenpoof Song, The, 117
Whiteman, Paul, 17, 24, 46
Whiteman, Wilberforce J., 17,
    39–40
Why can't we do it again, 87
Wilcox, Ed, 108

Williams, Joe, 1
Williams, John, 59, 70–71, 77, 114
Williams, Mayo, 73
Williams, Mary Lou, 51, 71, 72–3,
    110–11, 118
Williams, R. S., 42
Wilson, Dick, 103
With love in my heart, 87

You can take it from me, 61
Young, Johnny, 111
Young, Lester, 1